THE FILMS
OF
GINA
LOLLOBRIGIDA

THE FILMS
OF
GINA
LOLLOBRIGIDA

MAURICIO PONZI

translated from the Italian
by Shula Atil Curto
edited for the American edition
by Alvin H. Marill

CITADEL PRESS • SECAUCUS, NEW JERSEY

Foto Civirani, pages 7, 48 - Farabola, p. 8 bottom - G. B. Poletto, p. 13, 22, 28 top, 108, 109, 111 bottom, 118 - Chantal Sabria, p. 28 bottom - Robert and Raymond Hakim, p. 94 - Keystone, p. 97 - Foto Garofolo, p. 98 - Roma's Press Photo, p. 119 bottom - David Lascelles, p. 120 - A.F.P., p. 132 top.

The Author

Maurizio Ponzi was born in Rome on May 8, 1939. From 1962 to 1968, he was an editor of the magazine *Filmcritica* and has been co-editor of *Cinema & Film* and a contributor to *Cinema 60* and *Cahiers du Cinema*. In 1968, he directed his first film, *The Visionary*, which was followed by *Equinox* (1971) and *Raoul's Case* (1975). In 1972, he directed and edited, in collaboration with Pier Paolo Pasolini, *December 12th*. For television he has directed, among others, Stefano Junior (1969), *Eternal Day* (1970), *The Voice of Torture* (1973), *The Lost Years* (1978) and *Hedda Gabler* (1979). In the past decade, he directed a half-dozen successful films. This is his first book.

Acknowledgments

The author owes special thanks to Jean-Charles Sabria for generously supplying photographs. Without his help the book could never have been so amply documented.

Grateful thanks as well to Gianni Amelio, Enrico Lancia, Umberto Tani, Marcello Zago, Franco Castelnovi, Gaetano Strazzulla and the Roman bookshop Libreria dello Spettacolo.

The publisher has made every effort to credit the sources of all the photographs published in the book. Where no credit is offered, the publisher apologizes for error or omission. Correct credits will be presented in future editions.

Copyright © 1982 by Gremese Editore s.r.l.
Published by Citadel Press
A division of Lyle Stuart Inc.
120 Enterprise Ave., Secaucus, N.J. 07094
In Canada: Musson Book Company
A division of General Publishing Co. Limited
Don Mills, Ontario
Manufactured in the United States of America
ISBN 0-8056-1093-5

La Lollo

It is by no means a simple matter to write about Gina Lollobrigida the actress.

It is much easier to write about Gina Lollobrigida the star. But, can the two be separated? In Hollywood there would be little point, whereas in Italy they appear to be antithetical, though before going any further we perhaps should define the terms better. Is Alberto Sordi a star? Was Anna Magnani an actress? Or Totò an actor/star? If such terms are applied to Nino Manfredi or Ugo Tognazzi, or even to Jean Gabin, then they immediately seem to take on a derogatory tone. On the other hand, it is quite normal to apply them to certain social phenomena. Gina Lollobrigida is such a social phenomenon. In the Italian cinema, the difference between the actor of a theatrical background and the one whose career began on the screen has always been greater than elsewhere, especially during the early post-war years and indeed up until the end of the 1960s.

Neo-realism's dictate that "actors be taken from the street" derives essentially from the many dialects that exist in the Italian language, dialects that were absent from the language spoken by stage actors, who were widely employed, too widely perhaps, in pre-war Italian cinema. The "nouvelle vague" in Italy was really looking for faces whose physiognomy and expressiveness corresponded to a particular dialect. In fact, even though the criteria by which Vittorio De Sica chose Franco Interlenghi for *Sciuscià* and Maggiorani for *The Bicycle Thief* were different from those of Mario Costa when he approached Franca Marzi on a train and Gina Lollobrigida in Via Margutta. Both directors were prompted by the same motives when they engaged professional voices to dub their "finds." Actors or actresses, as the case may be, who were to prove all the more successful wherever they managed to identify with a distinct "type." The voice had to complement the screen personna. And Gina Lollobrigida is Italy's preeminent film star (Sophia Loren follows her, at least in chronological order), although throughout her career she tried tenaciously to gain recognition as an actress. We must, therefore, speak of both the star and the actress. We must analyze why this is such a typically Italian phenomenon, and why sometimes the two amalgamate offering Lollobrigida her greatest opportunities.

What triggered the Lollobrigida phenomenon?

"La Lollo", as she was affectionately called, saw her career commence in a way totally different from the usual Hollywood method of personality building. There was no advance planning, no publicity campaign, little professional advice. On the contrary, she was exploited, first hesitantly, then with increasing momentum, until her exploiters suddenly realized that she was like an untapped gold mine.

Gina's career began during the rebirth of the Italian cinema in the early post-war years. Many of the Italian actresses acquired fame and some international celebrity during the period. Few survived as "names" in the ensuing 20 years.

Alida Valli, beautiful and mysterious, scored nicely in several Italian films before shining briefly for David O. Selznick in Hollywood...Isa Miranda, "femme fatale," had a quick moment as star of both Italian and American films...and Valentina Cortese, the lovely and witty actress, also had a brief Hollywood career. Then there were the others, whose careers were even shorter. The luminous Luisa Ferida met with an early death. Clara Calamai, Mariella Lotti, Dina Sassoli and Elli Parvo were

About the time she made *Miss Italia* (1950).

With husband Milko Skofic in Venice in 1956.

quickly neglected. Forgotten too were Lilia Silvi, Irasema Dilian, Maria Denis and Adrianna Benetti. Of the male stars Amadeo Nazzari, Gino Servi, Massimo Girotti, Andrea Chocchi and, of course, Vittorio De Sica (both as actor and director) were to become internationally famous. Magnani, Loren Mastroiani, Vittorio Gassman and the comedian Toto made their screen debuts in late post-war years.

The Italian cinema needed new names for the "nouvelle vague," in which there was considerable scope for women. Women who had experienced the war, the resistance. But there was scope for beauty, too, for the girl whose beauty blazed her way to independence. Behind the beauty competition phenomenon, this chimera which hid an ages-old ideal (woman as a creature to admire and exploit), the young Italian girls were beginning to make a stand. Finally they could put into practice the things they had seen, and continued to see, in American films, a society model that even Fascism had adopted. The bikini and the household appliance, the swimming pool and the health resort, the big city and the talent scout, the front cover of a glossy magazine and travel to romantic places, a scantily covered bosom and a black "combinaison." These were the ingredients, some imported, some endemic, used to frame the florid, gushing beauty of the many starstruck young girls who aspired to a screen career.

Gina Lollobrigida's story begins here. She was the product of a modest background, serious-minded and of course extremely beautiful, like Silvana Mangano, Lucia Bosé and Anna Pampanini. But unlike that of her contemporaries, her road to success did not come easily and it was a long time before Gina was offered a part in anything but a minor film; on the other hand, she stubbornly refused to give up. Whereas Lucia Bosé, perhaps the most singular of Italian actresses of that period, hesitated, nagged by doubts as to whether to continue in her screen career, Gina Lollobrigida astutely did not lose sight of her goal. She always tried to please the public. She knew how to look after her own interests and she was well aware that she had no producer-husband to protect her, as did Silvana Mangano (and later Sophia Loren); she was careful to make no wrong moves, safeguarding that which fate or good fortune had given her. The adjectives chosen by Cardarelli to describe the particular beauty of Silvana Pampanini—"blooming, opulent, florid, typically Italian"—are just as true of Gina. She had a determination about her, the ability to gain the respect of the male of the species. Unlike that of Bosé, Mangano and Loren, all three of unquestionable grace and loveliness, "just as everything that is human and credible is beautiful" (wrote Pratolini), Gina's beauty is almost perfect. To the extent that it is almost unreal.

But then the "star system" needs even the unreal. In his article on the 1949 Locarno Film Festival, Adriano Baracco, editor of the magazines *Hollywood* and *Cinema*, wrote: "We just cannot ignore this amazing girl, who is so beautiful that she almost arouses our indignation. Whenever she walked by, all the men stared unbelievingly; even the women were disarmed by her. She has such a gentle air about her, at last people said, here is the perfect woman." Nobody ever doubted her perfection, but as far as her gentleness was concerned, many journalists were to give her a hard time in the years to come. Anyway, her beauty did not spoil her as a person. She has had an exemplary private life; a brief engagement, a quiet wedding in the mountain resort of Terminillo, near Rome, dressed in ski clothes.

It is significant that the other young actresses of this period had equally blameless lives: Silvana Mangano, married (to Dino DeLavrentiis) with a family; Lucia Bosé, a long engagement to actor Walter Chiari before her marriage to Spanish bull-fighter Dominguin which was to keep her away from the cinema for a while; Anna Pampanini, always accompanied by her father, never marrying. There were, as always, the nonconformists: Lea Padovani (a stormy affair with Orson Welles, which resulted in a momentary interruption in the filming of *Othello*), Anna Magnani (affairs with Alessandrini, Serato and Rossellini, not to mention her notorious quarrels with Ingrid Bergman), Alida Valli (a divorce).

One might argue that while these actresses were more accomplished in their work, they were fairly conventional in their private lives. As soon as these beauties became famous, they began downplaying their origins, the hated parade of the Miss Italy contest, and promised to dedicate their lives to "the art of cinema." One or two of them even repudiated their beauty: Silvana Mangano dieted rigorously in an effort to destroy the voluptuously sensual image she had created in *Riso amaro*. It was not until much later that "La Lollo" had a similar reaction, probably because success came much more slowly and for a long time she was just one among a myriad of voluptuous starlets.

Prior to 1952, the year of *Fanfan la Tulipe*, the actress had been offered, besides the ill-fated contract with Howard Hughes, roles that were totally unsuited to her particular talent. Sometimes she played the part of a modest, timid young girl (*Follie per l'opera*; *Amore non ho, però...però*; *Enrico Caruso*; *Achtung! Banditi!*; *Miss Italia*; *La sposa non può attendere*; *Cuori senza frontieri*), sometimes a victim (*Alina*), or a girl with ambitions (*Vita da cani*), or even a prostitute (*Campane a martello*).

Not that she failed to win recognition, luke-warm as it was and more often than not directly related to the success of the film itself. If we take a closer look at this early period in Gina's career we are inclined to be indulgent, and we must acknowledge that she was very good in at least *La città si difende*, *La sposa nonpuò attendere* and *Vita da cani*...good in the sense that she showed a natural inclination for being guided, and a natural, spontaneous rapport with the camera. Her beauty, tempered by the black and white photography and by the modest settings, is less startling. Of the people who directed her in those early years, Steno and Monicelli were perhaps the ones who best understood her character, when they offered her the role of Margherita in *Vita da cani*, an ambitious girl from a humble background, with a strong determination to make good. Certainly better than Duilio Coletti who, in *Miss Italia*, had her play the reluctant contest competitor whose only desire was to get married. But this was the case with most of the directors of Gina's early films. How it was that Christian-Jaque sensed Gina's natural vitality, offering her the part of Adeline in *Fanfan la Tulipe*, is something of a mystery and says much for this French director and for producer Peppino Amato. Once again it was the French who opened our Italian eyes, helping Gina to the success that had been so long in coming in this country. Not that she hadn't been noticed (as a matter of fact, the screen name of Sophia Loren was made up of the first two letters of Gina's surname, joined to the last letters of Marta Toren's), nor was she unknown to the public. It was however nothing compared with the burst of popularity that followed the presentation of *Fanfan la Tulipe* first at Cannes and then in Paris.

What then had changed? Adeline is an historical character, though "sui generis," and is both romantic and picaresque. And so Gina's unsurpassed beauty finally found the right environment in which to blossom forth, to be the only thing it could be: the most important feature of this star, one of Italy's first in post-war years.

The initial part of the struggle was thus over. Producers and directors alike had at last realized, and Gina too. With the exception of *Moglie per una notte*, the career of this new-born star flickered cautiously over a predetermined course.

Fanfan la Tulipe was followed by another hit; *Altri tempi*. It is a variation on a theme, a variation with diabolical undertones. Unlike Adeline, Mariantonia does not get excited, she does not gesticulate, does not run and leap around. She sits quietly in the dock, but the plunging neckline is the same and so is her knowing glance. Blasetti was very shrewd to have her sitting there while De Sica (as the lawyer) adroitly draws from her with his questions a response that in the end captures jury, judge and spectators.

In *Altri tempi*, the viewer, eager to enjoy the actress' exuberant charms, his imagination stimulated by the witnesses' testimonies, is ever conscious of an erotic vitality which has momentarily been dulled. The some feeling, more or less, that an ardent motor racing fan might experience to see a shining Maserati broken down. Then victory, Mariantonia is absolved, because it is not a crime to be beautiful— (physical majority) "maggiorata fisica", was De Sica's famous expression.

Once it had been established that beauty, because it can be denied or rationed, is an instrument of eroticism "par excellence," the time was ripe for *La provinciale*, an Albert Moravia story, a little ridiculous perhaps, about lower

Receiving the "Victoire" award in 1955.

On the set of *Fanfan la Tulipe* with Olivier Hussenot, Gérard Philipe, and Nerio Barnardi.

In *Pane, amore e fantasia* (1953).

At the 1955 Paris premiere of *Pane, amore e gelosia* with Robert Risso.

middle-class people. It is realistic, in the sense that it is neither picaresque nor farcical, the guide-line no longer being a "quid pro quo" as in *La sposa non può attendere*, or destiny as in *Alina*, or a social comment as in *Cuori senza frontieri*, but the unrequited sexual desires of a woman whose extreme beauty causes only trouble and anxiety. Neither the fake countess nor her vulgar client want Gemma. They lust for her body and care little for the fact that Gemma's body and soul are one. And as elsewhere in the cinema (from Bresson to Scorsese), the soul is represented by the body. *La provinciale* offered Gina the opportunity to create character. It was no longer a mere question of acting, of technique; it meant making a succession of episodes and a tumult of emotions seem credible. And Gina in *La provinciale*, whatever one might say about the film as a whole, did just this.

But because in the Italian cinema the dramatic film has generally taken second place to comedy, the success achieved by *La provinciale* was soon over-shadowed by that of *Pane, amore e fantasia*. At this point in her career, "La Lollo" made some very shrewd decisions. In 1952, she refused a role in *La signora senza camelie*, a difficult decision as it was no easy matter for the young Antonioni, at the start of his career, to make a film. Nonetheless, her decision was not unjustified. I am not familiar with the script that the actress refused (apparently, it was not that of the film that finally reached the screen, starring Lucia Bosé), but to have asked her to virtually destroy all that she had been trying to build up was asking too much.

By similar reasoning her appearance in John Huston's *Beat the Devil* was, from a commercial point of view, quite damaging to her image. But at least it was not quite as bad as it might have been, thanks to a prestigious cast headed by Bogart and in view of the recognition afforded the film in later years. It was another of those films that try to destroy a myth through irony, but perhaps it was too early in her career. Gina had been a star for too short a time. Some years later, when she appeared in a similiar role on television in Vittorio Gassman's *Il mattatore*, she was more successful.

There was also the minor *Il maestro di Don Giovanni*, which went virtually unnoticed. For most people Gina's next film, after *La provinciale*, was Comencini's *Pane, amore e fantasia*, as a simple country girl, rebellious and stubborn who, despite her poverty, is envied for her beauty and for this very reason is lusted after by the men of the village. The character is at once comical and pathetic, but totally straightforward. A triumph for neo-realism, but a romantic sort of neo-realism, a far cry from Emmer's *Domenica d'agosto* and Castellani's *Due soldi di speranza*, and it at last brought about a "reconciliation" of sorts between the Italian cinema and the public, which tired of seeing so many "ugly things" represented on the screen. Rarely was there, to this time, such an explicit film, and although De Sica's appearance might surprise some, given that he was one of the poets of those "ugly things," its popularity was enormous and Gina's personal triumph was without precedent for an Italian actress. Her photograph appeared on magazine covers, including throughout the world, *Time*, receptions were given in her honor by presidents and ambassadors and she was even received at the Court of St. James's. No longer was Italy's image oversees embodied in pizza, spaghetti and Loren alone; now there was also Gina Lollobrigida. Writer Filippo Sacchi once observed: "Her typically Italian beauty is like a blend of soft pasta and brightly colored sauce, just like our maccheroni!" adding, perhaps aware of just how touchy Gina can be: "It's meant to be a real compliment!"

While most of the world was talking about her, and in Italy the Lollo-Loren "battle" was furiously raging, the question "Who are you for, Coppi or Bartali? (soccer players) was countered by "Who do you prefer, La Lollo or La Loren?" It was a battle which many referred to as the "battle of the bosoms."

The young star, determined to become a truly professional actress, made a second film from a Moravia story: *La romana*. In comparison with Gemma of *La provinciale*, Adriana lives in a more complex world. A historical film, it is a story of fascists and anti-fascists, but despite Luigi Zampa's well-intentioned efforts, the character of Adriana, rather than moving within this environment, seems to be several steps ahead. Nonetheless, the film was enthusiastically greeted by critics

ITALY'S GINA LOLLOBRIGIDA
On the Tiber's banks, a new Hollywood.

SOME NEW MILLIONAIRES
HOW THEY GOT THAT WAY

GINA
NE OF ITALY'S
ERY BEAUTIES

20 CENTS

SEPTEMBER 3, 1951
CIRCULATION OVER
5,200,000

SIR ANTHONY—A NEW EDEN
A NEW CHANCE FOR EUROPE

GINA
LOBRIGIDA
R'S WARDROBE

20 CENTS
NOVEMBER 15, 1954

and audiences alike, and Gina could be well-satisfied that she had been accepted in the roles of both the "Bersagliera" and Moravia's Adriana. Few actresses have achieved this. She then took a step backwards in *Il grande gioco*, a mediocre film directed by Robert Siodmak at the end of his career. Many critics and writers offered their advice, as often happens when a national treasure puts a foot wrong.

But Gina was already at work on *Pane, amore e gelosia*, which she had finally agreed to make after some initial doubts, and rightly so, as it turned out. In reality, Comencini's film, despite its huge success, was just a pause in Gina's career, certainly not a step forward. And it was during this pause that the idea of making a film biography of Lina Cavalieri began to take shape.

La donna più bella del mondo provoked the first note of discord between Italy's biggest star and the critics, who had up until that moment encouraged, protected and advised her. That it was a bad film can be more easily forgotten than the fact that it was built up around a gross presumption; in fact, they virtually did without a director, American veteran Robert Z. Leonard's contribution as such being negligible. Strangely enough, the film was a hit. Evidently, Gina had realized that the public wanted to see the "Bersagliera" make good, wear beautiful clothes, make love to Russian princes in grand palaces and landscaped gardens, even hear her sing *Tosca* arias. *La donna più bella del mondo*, a true "Lollobrigida vehicle," was in reality the prelude to a radical change in the actress's career, one that was to keep her away from Italian cinema for several years. The dream she had been nurturing ever since the ill-fated Howard Hughes episode suddenly became reality with *Trapeze*.

"La Lollo's" American interlude, like Sophia Loren's, was different from those of Isa Miranda, Alida Valli, Valentina Cortese and Rossano Brazzi, whom Hollywood had tried to mold to its own image, as indeed it had done with several other non-American actresses (Dietrich, Garbo, Bergman, and in post-war years, Jean Simmons and Deborah Kerr, just to name a few). Hollywood bought Gina already packaged so to speak, with "Made in Italy" stamped across her in capital letters, and then integrated her into the system. The results of this operation were, as we shall see, varied. First of all, though, it should be pointed out that Gina's decision to leave Italy even temporarily was seen by many of her fans as a real betrayal. Toward herself and toward the Italian cinema which had, it must be admitted, given her four or five big hits, four or five roles tailor-made for her particular talent, and which Hollywood could never have offered her. On the other hand, apart from the dollars, America promised an international career and an organization which, perfectionist as she was, she had been unable to find in her own country. While Italians saw her picture in movie magazine after movie magazine, as she waved smilingly from aircraft gangways en route to and from the United States, Gina herself was busy improving her English, playing Lola in *Trapeze* and Esmeralda in *Notre Dame de Paris*. And it was during this period that her son Milko Junior was born (the announcement and press conference in her villa on the Appian Way was a major event!). She persuaded De Sica to accept a role in *Anna di Brooklyn* and she also signed a contract for two MGM films and three with United Artists, not to mention playing Marietta in *La legge* (The Law).

Few of these films achieved the success of her Italian days, and despite the rather questionable *Go Naked in the World*, Gina did enhance her talent as a comedienne, as is evident in the two movies with Rock Hudson as well as those with Bob Hope and Alec Guinness, and several Italian movies of the 1960s: *Le bambole*; *To, io, io…e gli altri*; *Mare matto*, for instance. But one fact remained: the image of Gina created by the public survived all attempts at modification. This image was evoked more by the press and glossy magazines than by her new movies. Her meeting with the American astronauts and her separation from Milko Skofic were her more publicized performances, and her moving her residence to Canada was given more attention than her latest American film! A similar state of affairs can be fatal to a star striving to become an actress. What was needed at this point was something out of the ordinary, a new and very special part. Perhaps the role of Emma in Fellini's *La dolce vita*, a role well-suited to Gina's physical

In Delannoy's *Notre Dame de Paris* (1956).

attributes, of a 30-year-old woman, both material and sensual at the same time, if not actually erasing from the public's mind the image of the "Bersagliera," might at least have gained her recognition as an actress. As it was, upon her return from Hollywood, she was offered parts in films of a very different level: *La bellezza di Ippolita* and *Venere imperiale*. The first was enjoyable enough, but mere routine for the actress. The second was a repeat of the *La donna più bella del mondo* formula, though Jean Delannoy's film is better made than Leonard's and it has a more accomplished cast. The film was very popular and Gina received not only praise but an award too.

The second phase of Gina's career was marked by an international fame and popularity similar to her early years, and which continued ten years or so after her retirement from the screen. Of the 1960s, the following are perhaps her best films: *Buona Sera, Mrs. Campbell*, a lively movie, competently acted; *To, io, io…e gli altri*, in which she starred beside Walter Chiari in a role well-fitted to her personality, and Skolimowski's *King, Queen, Knave*, her last good film to date. But the truth is that "La Lollo" was perhaps too much a star for just any film. Which was a pity because, whatever the critics may have written about her, Gina in her post-Hollywood period would certainly have been able to hold her own beside the

With Giustino Durano, Stephen Boyd and an unidentified actress in Dolannoy's *Venere imperiale* (1962).

bigger names of Italian comedy, such as Manfredi, Tognazzi and Sordi. It is both surprising and unfortunate that an actress who so untiringly had sought to manifest her professionalism and progress should suddenly have been excluded from the better efforts of the Italian cinema.

It is difficult to comment on the last movies she made. With the exception perhaps of Skolimowski's film, which began well enough but which was in the end abandoned by its director, who refused to have anything further to do with the editing. In addition to this, several modifications were made to the film before it reached, after a three-year delay, Italian screens. And with the exception, of course, of Comencini's charming *Le avventure di Pinocchio*, in which Gina plays the "Fata Turchina," a girl with blue hair. What fairy tale is more Italian than Pinocchio? And what beauty is more Italian than Gina Lollobrigida? She was the perfect fairy, and how well she acted, but did she realize it? In recent years, she has devoted herself to a new activity, but the public has not forgotten her. Recently, during a television show *Flash*, she was voted "Italy's most enchanting woman." She had won yet another beauty competition; an act of loyalty on the part of the jury to the myths and twists of fate of the motion picture world, an art which, though showing us "death at work" also renders so much life, so much extra time.

Leaving for New York from Orly in 1960 with husband Milko Skofic.

With Paolo Turco in *Un bellissimo novembre* (1968).

15

An Interview with "La Lolla"

Q. What was your reaction the first time you were approached in the street and asked if you would like to be in a film?

A. I was not in the slightest bit interested in the cinema at that time, as I was studying at the Academy of Fine Arts and taking singing lessons, too. My dream was to become a soprano. I agreed to be an extra in *Aquila Nera* because the war had only just ended and I needed money to pay for my singing lessons. I had won a scholarship to the Academy, so that was no problem. I was really quite indifferent toward the cinema, as a possible career, that is. But I did make a few photo-novels and worked as an extra in films, I even had a few minor roles, anything to help my family. When Mario Costa first asked me to play the lead in *I pagliacci*, I refused. A week later, after he had screen-tested a number of other actresses, he came back trying to get me to change my mind. At the time I was earning 1000 lire a day for each appearance. I asked him for one million, quite certain that he would refuse. To my surprise, he agreed.

Q. Was this when you seriously decided to become an actress?

A. No. It was not a hasty decision at all. At the back of my mind as I worked in films was the thought that I could always go back to my first loves: painting and singing. But even in those early days I was eager to express myself and the cinema gave me this opportunity, even though you were conditioned by your director, the story, the producer, a whole organization, in fact.

Q. What about the beauty competitions?

A. A friend persuaded me to enter the Miss Rome contest because the first prize was an accordian. I did not take it very seriously and I came in second. Then they wanted me to represent Rome in the Miss Italy competition in Stresa.

Q. Was it about this time that you signed a contract with Carlo Ponti for three films?

A. I do not remember exactly, but they cannot have been very important films. I would hardly say that I had an easy climb to the top, because it was not until 1952 that I made *Fanfan la Tulipe*, the movie that finally gave me international success.

Q. Yes, but let us talk about the early films anyway, about Ponti and Aldo Fabrizi.

A. I must admit, it was not easy working with Fabrizi; he was a bit of a dictator. As for Carlo Ponti, well, he spent most of his time complaining about Italian actresses—how they had no preparation, how they could not sing, could not dance, just the opposite of the Hollywood actresses. The truth is that in those days, and still today, there was a great deal of improvisation. Sometimes, this can produce good results. Personally, I prefer to work with a minimum of organization, as is the case in America, consequently the acting profession enjoys greater respect there.

Q. When Howard Hughes approached you in 1951, did you accept at once?

A. I had been in Hollywood two months when I signed a seven-year contract with Howard Hughes. But then there was the question of Hughes wanting me to divorce my husband and marry him, and my husband was understandably jealous, so I left the States soon after.

Q. Quite rightly, you attach much importance to *Fanfan la Tulipe*. How did you meet Christian-Jaque?

In Christian-Jaque's *Fanfan la Tulipe* (1951).

A. Thanks to Giuseppe Amato, because the film was co-produced. I have happy memories of that movie. Gérard Philipe was very kind to me and helped me with my French. And he was a good actor, too. The atmosphere on the set was good-humored and relaxed.

Q. As you can see. It is certainly a light-hearted film.

A. The film was about to be released when the French suddenly realized that "Lollo" in their language meant "big bosom." They asked me to change my surname! I told them I would have been pleased to do so, only the credits were all ready, so they had to abandon the idea. The surname became so famous that a new adjective was invented: "Lollobrigi dienne," which means roughly "aux formes sculpturales."

Q. How and when did you first realize that you had become a "star"?

A. If by "star" you mean "popular actress," then let me just say this. The film had only been showing one week in the Champs-Elysées, when the distributors had all the bills re-printed, with my name larger than Gérard Philipe's. My picture was bigger than the buildings on the poster even. And strange to say, there had been no big advertising campaign. The public dictated my success, quite spontaneously. Perhaps that is why my popularity has lasted so long. It was not "invented."

Q. How did success affect you?

A. I was a bit afraid of it, quite honestly. I have never really come to terms with my popularity, and it has always made me feel ill at ease.

Q. People remember you as being a very cautious person, to the point of being almost diffident. How true is it?

A. The motion picture profession is not an easy one. If it is the director who makes the decisions, then why should not we, the actors and actresses, have a right to defend ourselves. I am not diffident, just a professional. And there is not one producer who could deny it. I have on many occasions asked for my part in a film to be altered. I have done so whenever I thought it necessary in the interests of the film, as any professional would have done.

Q. So this is the secret of your success?

A. Professionalism, love for and dedication to my work, these are essentials, but talent and a fair share of good luck are equally important to get you to the top.

Q. Going back to your career, 1952 was the year of *Altri tempi*.

A. Quite delightful. I remember De Sica,Blasetti and I all had a hard time trying not to laugh during filming. And it was a good experience for me not to play a dramatic role for once.

Q. Then came Soldati's *La provinciale*, one of your best roles, I believe?

A. It was a difficult role, it is true, and one that everybody liked. I liked it less, however.

Q. Why?

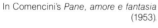
In Comencini's *Pane, amore e fantasia* (1953).

A. Because I have done better. I am a severe critic of my own work. I tend to concentrate on the faults rather than the merits.

Q. I believe you dubbed yourself for the first time in *La provinciale*. This must have meant a lot to you?

A. Yes. I had finally managed to persuade the producers not to allow the dubbing team to do just what they wanted, as is so often the case. How many times have we heard the voices of famous American singers dubbed into Italian? They would not have thought twice about dubbing me, a newcomer to the scene. But as I said before, unfortunately, Italy is a country of improvisation. Rarely has a film a perfect soundtrack, the policy being: "Well, the dubbing team can put it right." I have even known them to rewrite the dialogue from start to finish. I really had to put my foot down once; in dubbing a film I had made in English, they wanted to add a string of swear words, arguing that this would be appreciated by "certain" audiences! This is why, right from the early years, I always insisted that a clause be added to my contract stipulating that my voice was not to be dubbed by somebody else in either Italian, French or English.

Q. Then came *Pane, amore e fantasia*.

A. I signed the contract with Comencini, but the film was actually directed by De Sica, as was *Pane, amore e gelosia*. There was no secret about it, everybody knew.

Q. Did you realize right away that the character of the "Bersagliera" was going to become as popular as she did?

A. Much depended on the fact that De Sica was directing and the "Bersagliera" herself was a person of many subtleties, ranging from the comical to the dramatic. A humane, strong, real character. I would not have been able to create her without the help of De Sica, one of the best directors I have ever met. In Italy, at least, this is perhaps the best remembered of my films. Whereas abroad it was *Buona Sera, Mrs. Campbell,* which enjoyed much the same popularity.

Q. And Zampa's *La romana*?

A. That was a difficult, dramatic role and Zampa was an excellent director. It was undoubtedly a very useful experience for me.

Q. Then you went to France again for *Il grande giuoco*?

A. To be quite honest, I remember nothing about it at all.

Q. Why did you agree to make *Pane, amore e gelosia*?

A. Because De Sica was very insistent! It is one of my principles not to exploit a previous success. In fact, I did refuse to make a third film of the series and did something quite different instead: *La donna più bella del mondo,* which might not have been a masterpiece, but it beat all box-office records that year.

Q. In the film, you actually sing arias from *Tosca*.

A. Quite right. When the film was released in France, it received some enthusiastic reviews from *Le Figaro,* but they added: "What a pity it is not Lollobrigida's real voice"! *The New York Times* wrote the same thing. Nobody could believe that I had such a good singing voice.

Q. But the credits made it clear that it really was you singing?

A. Even the critics make mistakes sometimes, do they not?

Q. But that was the only time you ever sang in a film, I believe.

A. To follow two careers at the same time would have been practically impossible. I had many offers to sing on Broadway and still get them. But it is one thing to sing a song or two like I did, quite another to sing every evening. As yet I have not allowed temptation to get the better of me.

Q. What do you remember about *Beat the Devil*?

A. The critics really hit it, not just in Italy, but everywhere. It was released a second time ten years later and had quite a different reception. Even the experts judged it to be an excellent film! Written by such a well-known novelist as Truman Capote, people just did not understand the movie when it was first shown, because it was ahead of its time. Now it is considered a classsic of contemporary cinema.

Q. Then with the Americans you made *Trapeze*.

A. Together with *Buona Sera, Mrs. Campbell,* this is perhaps the best remembered, best loved of all my films.

Q. Delannoy must be another of your favorite directors?

A. Yes, indeed, and I have worked with him on three films. The most important of these was *Venere imperiale.* Paolina is an extraordinary character and Renato Castellani's script was one of the best I have ever read.

Q. How do you feel today about your refusal to star in Antonioni's *La signora senza camelie*?

A. Exactly how I felt then. It was a caricature of Italian cinema. I would have been ridiculing the world in which I worked, The producers I knew, the actresses, Silvana Mangano, my friends and myself. I asked for the script to be altered, but I was told it was too late and so I decided not to do it.

Q. But I would not have said the film was offensive.

A. The film that finally reached the screens was not, in fact. I would not have refused to do it, had they shown me that particular script. It is very different from the one I read.

Q. I see. Anyway, do you regret not having worked with Antonioni?

With Jean-Claude Pascal in Siodmak's *Il grande gioco* (1954).

Parading the streets of Paris with Tony Curtis, Katy Jurado and Burt Lancaster to launch their film *Trapeze* in 1956.

With Ralph Richardson in Dearden's *Woman of Straw* (1963).

A. I respected him, which is why I had agreed to work with him in the first place.

Q. Going back to your films, next came *Solomon and Sheba*.

A. I remember it well because of the death of Tyrone Power. It was a terrible experience, especially as I was so young at the time.

Q. At what point was the film when it happened?

A. There were only two more weeks to go and they were all scenes with just Tyrone and myself. There was nothing we could do but shoot the entire movie again with Yul Brynner.

Q. Do you consider yourself more a dramatic actress or a comedienne?

A. I have always had more offers for comedies. Castellani, for whom I have the greatest respect, offered me quite a different part in *Mare matto*. I think that was perhaps my best dramatic role.

Q. And your best comedy?

A. *Buona Sera, Mrs. Campbell* and Skolimowskyi's *King, Queen, Knave*, the last film I made.

Q. Did you ever feel that you were being offered a role more for your looks than for your talent?

A. It has happened. Not often do people, audiences and critics alike, acknowledge talent in a beautiful woman. They are more likely to be put off by beauty with intelligence. It is much easier to dream about a woman with no ideas of her own, no personality...a doll, an object.

Q. In other words, your beauty has sometimes hindered rather than helped you?

A. No, it has helped me, because the cinema needs expressive faces. But I see no point in discussing it now.

Q. Famous as you are, how come you have been away from the cinema for so long?

A. I enjoyed making films as long as I was being offered good scripts. You cannot be in this profession for over 30 years without giving it your heart. In later years, I was looking for more demanding roles but unfortunately none were offered me. But I was not the only Italian actress with this problem. It is far from easy today to find a worthwhile script and a good director, so I did not have to think twice about leaving motion pictures when I took up photography.

Q. Tell us about this new interest of yours?

A. It started as a hobby and slowly became a profession, to gratify this need I felt to discover and create. Photography is rather like directing, moreover you are free to make your own decisions. Art helps me to express myself to the full.

Q. What about the future? Is there any chance of your going back to the cinema?

A. I hope so. In the meantime, I have directed two documentaries, one about Fidel Castro, the other about the Philippines. I might even appear on Broadway, but photography will always be an important part of my life.

With Argentina Brunetti in *Buona Sera, Mrs. Campbell* (1968).

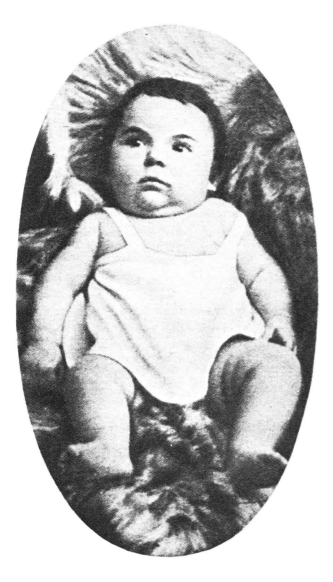

Gina at seven months (left).

At the age of five (first on the left) with her mother Giuseppina, father Giovanni and two sisters (top).

At 13 in a snapshot vaguely reminiscent of the "Bersagliera" in *Pane, amore e fantasia* (bottom left).

Ten-year-old Gina (sitting) with sisters Giuliana (standing on right) age 13, Maria (on the left) age 4, and Fernanda age 2.

Curriculum Vitae

1927-1928—Luigina was born on July 4th at Subiaco, in the Lazio region near Rome, the daughter of Giovanni Lollobrigida, owner of a small carpentry business, and Giuseppina Mercuri. She had three sisters, Giuliana, Maria and Fernanda.

1935—She made her stage debut, dressed as a little sailor boy, with a company of amateur actors. But it was only an excuse for a day off school and had no follow-up.

1944—The Lollobrigida family moved to Todi.

1945—The war over, the family moved again, this time to Rome, where they rented a room in Via Taranto, near to Porta San Giovanni. Gina's father was unemployed and the early months were hard. Giuliana and Maria found work as usherettes at the cinema, while Gina, for a few lire, sketched caricatures and portraits of American GIs.

1946—Things began to improve for the family. They moved to an apartment in Via Montebello, and Gina won a scholarship to the Academy of Fine Arts. One day, Stefano Canzio stopped her in the street and asked her if she would like to be a film extra. Gina agreed, knowing that the extra money would help pay for her singing lessons, her true ambition being a career in opera. And so her very first screen appearance was in Riccardo Freda's *Aquila Nera*.

1947—It was New Year's Eve when Gina met Milko Skofic, the man she was to marry. She was again stopped in the street and offered a part in a film, this time Mario Costa's *L'elisir d'amore*. Her pay was 15,000 lire, plus overtime bringing it up to 40,000. She spent it all on a new coat and umbrella! She appeared in several other films that year and also signed a contract to "star" in a "photo-romance" for the magazine *Il mio sogno* (later to become *Sogno*, which is still published). The story was entitled "In fondo al cuore" ("At the Bottom of My heart") and ran over 22 episodes, from May 3rd (first edition of the magazine) to October 5th 1947. She starred with the name Gina Loris. In the summer, she entered the Miss Rome competition and came in second to a Sicilian girl named Niní du Bac. Gina was then invited to take Niní's place in the Miss Italy contest held that year in Stresa, where she found herself competing against Lucia Bosé, Gianna Maria Canale and Eleonora Rossi (later to become Rossi Drago). The title was won by Lucia, with Gianna Maria second and Gina third.

The day of her first communion.

1948—Although she had not actually won the Miss Italy contest, it was through this popular competition that Gina found her next engagement. Mario Costa offered her parts in two of his films: *Follie per l'opera* and *I pagliacci*. Audiences and critics alike began to take notice of her.

1949—On January 4th, she and Milko Skofic were married in the church at Terminillo, a ski resort near Rome. Both bride and groom wore ski outfits, and one

With American writer Truman Capote, one of her dearest friends and admirers. Below, an eloquent dedication to Gina.

-oR Gina
a great
antist —
and an aToToTh
special —
antist —
Truman Capote

With De Sica in Comencini's *Pane, amore e fantasia* (1953).

of the witnesses was Yvonne Sanson. Gina and Milko set up house in Via Sambucuccio d'Alando near Piazza Bologna. Milko was a doctor but gave up his profession soon afterward to manage his wife's career. It was during this period that Gina had been engaged by Carlo Ponti, later to marry Gina's "rival," Sophia Loren. It was also the year of *Campane a martello*, *La sposa non può attendere*, *Miss Italia* and *Cuori senza frontieri*, all good films of their kind, yet none offered Gina the role that was to set her on the road to stardom.

1950—Two popular films: *Alina* and *Vita da cani*. The latter was particularly successful and the offers began to increase. She was invited to Hollywood by producer Howard Hughes. Her trip paid for by RKO, she left unaccompanied on June 22nd for Los Angeles. Once there, she signed a seven-year contract with Hughes and eagerly started learning English. But her husband wanted her back in Rome, and in October, Gina gave in to his entreaties and went home. Despite her contract and Hughes' urgings, this was the end of Gina's Hollywood interlude, at least for the time being.

1951—Gina played a minor role in *La città si difende*, presented at the Venice Film Festival and then agreed to star in *Achtung! Banditi!*, a film produced by a cooperative. But it was with a less ambitious movie that Gina finally met with the success she deserved, Gentilomo's *Enrico Caruso, leggenda di una voce*. And after this she was chosen by Christian-Jaque to star opposite Gérard Philipe in *Fanfan la Tulipe*. The film, shown at Cannes, was enormously popular in France and equally successful in Italy.

1952—Gina was directed by Vittorio De Sica in an episode of Blasetti's *Altri tempi*. It was another triumph and it was from this film that the term "maggiorata fisica" came! "La Lollo's" plunging neckline was the conversation piece of Italians everywhere. In the fashion world, Gina's bust was the model to be copied. Then it was back to France to make *Les belles de nuit*, again with Gérard Philipe. The film was shown at that year's Venice Film Festival. There could be no further doubt, Gina Lollobrigida was a star. That same year, she agreed to make *La signora senza camelie* for Antonioni, whose aim it was to destroy certain false myths about the Italian movie world. In the belief that the original script put her, and many colleagues, in a bad light, Gina asked that certain modifications be made. Her request was refused and she walked out the day before shooting was to begin. The role was offered to Lucia Bosé, who gave a fine performance, though her physique was not exactly what the film required. In all events, legal proceeding went on for some time afterward.

1953—Gina was engaged by Sam Spiegel for John Huston's *Beat the Devil*. For the first time, Gina had to speak on screen in English and share it with such famous names as Humphrey Bogart, Jennifer Jones, Peter Lorre and Robert Morley. The dialogue was written by Truman Capote, who was to become a firm friend of Gina's. But it was not until ten years later, in 1963, when released for the second time, that Huston's film found its audience. Next came *Il maestra di Don Giovanni,* an Errol Flynn swashbuckler, Gina's first color film. Another hit was *La provinciale*, taken from a story by Alberto Moravia, which won Gina a "Grolla d'oro." But 1953 was, above all, the year of *Pane, amore e fantasia*, her greatest and longest lasting success. The box office was outstanding and the critics were united in their praise of her acting. Moreover, the film won a "Nastro d'argento." By now, Gina was Italy's highest paid actress. She was invited to the White House, The Court of St. James's, by Juan Peron and the Shah of Iran. She was described as Italy's ambassadress of beauty.

1954—Gina had to refuse Blasetti's offer to star in *Tempi nostri*, due to a previous agreement with Zampa for *La romana*, an interesting movie that was shown at that year's Venice Film Festival. After this, she returned to France for the remake of *Il grande gioco*. She hesitated over again playing the "Bersagliera" in *Pane, amore e gelosia*, but finally agreed and the film went on to become an even bigger box office hit than the first of the series. In New York, Gina had occasion to meet Marilyn Monroe, who told her: "You know, they call me America's Lollobrigida!"

1955—Gina could not be persuaded to make the third film of the series, *Pane, amore e....* Instead she starred in and co-produced *La donna più bella del mondo*, a biography of Lina Cavalieri. In it she sang a number of songs and even an aria from "Tosca." Although the film was hardly embraced by the critics, it was the biggest box office hit of the season.

1956—Still under contract to Hughes, Gina went to Paris to make an American film, the influence of this mythical magnate being somewhat more tenuous in the French capital! The movie was *Trapeze*, in which she co-starred with Burt Lancaster, Tony Curtis and Katy Jurado. Carol Reed directed. Another hit. And it was in France again where Gina made her next film, Jean Delannoy's rather oppressive, melancholy version of *Notre Dame de Paris* with Anthony Quinn.

1957—On July 28th, Milko Junior was born.

1958—Back to motion pictures to star in *Anna di Brooklyn*, a film produced by her husband Milko Skofic and "supervised," but in reality directed, by De Sica. After this she joined the cast of *La legge*. Expatriate American director Jules Dassin had been having difficulty in finding the lead actress. Gina was somewhat older than the character in the book and the script had to be modified accordingly. The role of the agronomist was developed too, and offered to Marcello Mastroianni.

With Milko Junior a few days after his birth.

1959—Gina was at last free to return to Hollywood where she made three films. Two were for MGM: *Never So Few* and *Go Naked in the World*, and one for United Artists: *Solomon and Sheba*, which actually was shot in Spain. This last film was marked by the untimely death of actor Tyrone Power before shooting had been completed. Yul Brynner was called in to take the role and the film had to be virtually remade. Gina then screen-tested for the lead in Martin Ritt's *Yovanka elle altre* (the part ultimately was played by Mangano). And apparently she was also offered the part of Emma in Fellini's *La dolce vita* and of the heroine in Bunuel's *Viridiana*. She also made her debut on Italian television in an episode of Vittorio Gassman's *Il mattatore*, in which she gave a delightful parody of a movie star.

In Zagni's *La bellezza di Ippolita* (1962).

1961—Gina was engaged by Universal to make *Come September* with Rock Hudson, which was filmed partly in Italy. Of all her Hollywood movies, this was the biggest box office hit.

1962—For Giancarlo Zagni's first film *La bellezza di Ippolita*, Gina went blonde. Next came a much coveted role, that of Paolina Borghese in *Venere imperiale*, a film that won her a great deal of acclaim—another "Nastro d'argento" and a "David di Donatello."

1963—Castellani created a quite different role for Gina—an unattractive, avaricious woman in *Mare matto*, and she handled the challenge well. Next, it was off to England to make *Woman of Straw* with Sean Connery.

1964—Again, Gina starred opposite Rock Hudson in Melvin Frank's comedy *Strange Bedfellows* and then it was back to Italy to make an episode directed by Bolognini of *Le bambole*.

1966—Gina and Milko Skofic were separated. Under the direction of Blasetti, Gina next made *Io, io, io....e gli altri*. She then went to France (Delannoy's *L'amante italiana*), England (Peter Glenville's *Hotel Paradise*) and Spain (Vincent Sherman's *Cervantes*).

With Jean-Charles Sabria (left) and Jean Delannoy at an exhibition of her photographs in 1980.

1967—After playing the female lead role in Questi's *La morte ha fatto l'uovo*, it was off to America again for a guest appearance in Frank Tashlin's *The Private Navy of Sgt. O'Farrell* starring Bob Hope. This film was not released in Italy until 1975.

1968—It was yet another Hollywood-made movie that put Gina back on the road to success—Melvin Frank's *Buona Sera, Mrs. Campbell*, perhaps her best known film outside of Italy, *Pane, amore e fantasia* notwithstanding. And it won her a "David di Donatello." Following this, she was back working with Bolognini in *Un bellissimo novembre*. There were problems, and for the first time for 15 years Gina was obliged to agree to her voice being dubbed.

1969—Although it was a minor Italian film, Gina found *Stuntman* an enjoyable experience, as she was able to design her own costumes. She was then involved in a rather serious road accident and confined to her bed for several months. To shake off the apathy of a prolonged period of convalescence, she agreed to appear in a TV special entitled *Stasera Gina Lollobrigida*, in which she danced, sang and gave impersonations of famous women.

1970—This was the year of Gina's only western, the Spanish-made *Bad Man's River*, with James Mason.

1971—Gina was asked by director Luigi Comencini to play the role of the blue-haired girl in the Italian television production of *Le avventure di Pinocchio*. This highly acclaimed production was released theatrically in Italy one year later and then was repeated on television in 1975 and again in 1981. In April, Gina was legally divorced.

1972—Two films marked Gina's voluntary retirement from motion pictures, first Skolimowski's *King, Queen, Knave*, taken from the Vladimir Nabokov novel, and then a minor Spanish film, *Peccato mortale*. That same year, she published a book entitled *Italia mia*, which won the Nadar award. She also directed two documentaries: *Ritratto di Fidel* and *Le Filippine*, published two photographick documentaries: *Manila* and *The Philippines*, and had her photographs exhibited in countries throughout the world.

1973-1982—During this period, Gina dedicated most of her time to her photography, which by now had grown from a hobby to a true profession. In October 1980, she organized an exhibition in Paris and won the Vermeil award. In recent years she has devoted herself to executive work at fashion and cosmetic firms.

1984—Gina made her American televison acting debut in a recurring role as Francesca Gioberti in "Falcon Crest".

1985—In her first TV movie, Gina plays wealthy Princess Alexandra in the two-part adaptation of Judith Micheals' novel *Deception*, starring Stéfanie Powers.

THE FILMS

Aquila Nera

1946

Produced by DCI. Director: Riccardo Freda. From the story *Dubrovsky* by Alexandr Pushkin. Screenplay: Mario Monicelli, Steno, Riccardo Freda. Photography: Rodolfo Lombardi (b/w). Music: Franco Casavola. Art director: Arrigo Equini. Editor: Otello Colangeli. Distribution: DCI. Running time: 112 minutes. French title: *L'aigle noir.* English title: *The Black Eagle.* American title: *Return of the Black Eagle.*

CAST

Rossano Brazzi (Vladimir Dubrowsky), Irasema Dilian (Masha), Gino Cervi (Kirila), Rina Morelli (Irene), Harry Feist (Prince Sergei), Paolo Stoppa (Bandit), Inga Gort (Maria), Luigi Pavese (a servant), Pietro Sharoff, Angelo Calabrese, Cesare Polacco.

In this adaptation of the Pushkin novel about a Russian officer who vows vengeance on a ruthless landowner, Gina Lollobrigida appears in a party scene with a group of other young girls, among them Yvonne Sanson.

At Cinecittà during a pause in the filming of *Aquila nera.*

Lucia di Lammermoor

1946

Produced by Opera Film. Director: Piero Ballerini. From the opera by Gaetano Donizetti based on the novel by Sir Walter Scott, set to a story by Salvatore Cammarano. Screenplay: Piero Ballerini and Pier Giuseppe Franci. Photography: Mario Albertelli (b/w). Conductor: Oliviero De Fabritiis. Art Director: Carlo Egidi. Costumes: Flavio Mogherini. Editor: Renzo Lucidi. Origin: Italy. Running time: 108 minutes.

CAST

Nelly Corradi (Lucia), Afro Polo (Lord Ashton), Mario Filippeschi (Sir Edgar), Aldo Ferracuti (Lord Bucklaw), Italo Tajo (Raymond Bidebent), Loretta Di Lelio (Alisa), Adelio Zagonara (Norman).

Gina Lollobrigida again is no more than an extra.

Il segreto di Don Giovanni (The Secret of Don Giovanni)

1947

Produced by Pegoraro for Scalera Productions. Directed by Camillo Mastrocinque.* Screenplay: Aldo Calvo.** Photography: Arturo Gallea. Music: Fernando Previtali. Editor: Fernando Tropea. Distribution: 20th Century-Fox. Origin: Italy. American title: *When Love Calls*.

CAST

Gino Bechi (Claudio Tancredi), Silvana Pampanini (Anna Tancredi), Gino Saltamerenda (Squarcione), Liliana Laine (Emmy), Aroldo Tieri (Pacini), Carlo Romano (Maestro Marconi), Mario Siletti, Checco Durante.

BACKGROUND AND REVIEWS

This is the film in which Silvana Pampanini made her screen debut, but Gina is still only an unbilled extra. "[It] is eminently qualified to discourage the average moviegoer from ever wanting to see another Italian film." (Bosley Crowther, *The New York Times*, 9 October 1948).

*Both the *Annuario del cinema italiano* and the *Catalogo Bolaffi* mistakenly name Mario Costa as director of the film.

**Variety* and *The New York Times* both credit Vittorio Novarese with the screenplay.

Il Delitto di Giovanni Episcopo (The Crime of Giovanni Episcopo)

1947

Produced by Marcello D'Amico for Lux Film-Pao. Director: Alberto Lattuada. From the story *Giovanni Episcopo* by Gabriele D'Annunzio. Screenplay: Suso Cecchi D'Amico, Federico Fellini, Aldo Fabrizi, Piero Tellini. Photography: Aldo Tonti (b/w). Music: Felice Lattuada. Art Director: Guidi Fiorini. Costumes: Gino Sensani. Editors: Mario Bonotti and Guiliana Attenni. Distribution: Lux Film. Origin: Italy. French title: *Le Crime de Giovanni Episcopo*. American title: *Flesh Will Surrender*. Title during filming: *Pensione California*.

CAST

Aldo Fabrizi (Giovanni Episcopo), Yvonne Sanson (Ginevra), Rolando Lupi (Giulio Wanzer), Ave Ninchi (Emilia), Jone Morino (Signora Canale), Nando Bruno (Antonio), Alberto Sordi (Doberti), Francesco De Marco (Canale), Lia Grani (Adele), Gino Cavalieri (archivist), Gian Luca Cortese (Marquis Agulfi), Amedeo Fabrizi (Ciro), Maria Gonnelli (Santina), Giorgio Moser, Marco Tulli, Folco Lulli, Galeazzo Benti, Ferrante Alvaro De Torres, Gilberto Severi, Diego Calcagno, Silvano Mangano, Gina Lollobrigida.

BACKGROUND AND REVIEWS

Gina Lollobrigida appears, together with Silvana Mangano, in a New Year's Eve party scene. Lattuada remembers having shown her in close-up. It also was to be the closest Lollobrigida ever came to working with Fellini, here one of the screenwriters. "*Flesh Will Surrender* and it does here, but no spectator in his right mind will." (Howard Thompson, *The New York Times*, 27 October 1950).

Vendetta nel sole (A Man About the House)

1947

Produced by Edward Black for Excelsa Film-London Film. Directors: Leslie Arliss and Giuseppe Amato. Screenplay: J.B. Williams and Giuseppe Amato from a story by Francis Brett Young and a play by John Perry. Photography: George Perinal. Music: Nicholas Brodzsky. Art directors: G. Santangelo and T. B. Williams. Distribution: Minerva Film. Origin: Italy/ Great Britain. French title: *Un homme dans la maison*. Title during filming: *Delitti a Ravello*. Running time: 88 minutes.

Dulcie Gray (Ellen Isit), Margaret Johnston (Agnes Isit), Kieron Moore (Salvatore), Guy Middleton (Sir Benjamin Dench), Felix Aylmer (Richard Sanctuary), Jone Solinas (Maria), Maria Fimiani (Assunta), Reginald Purdell (Higgs), Lillian Braithwaite (Mrs. Armitage), Fedele Gentile, Fulvia de Priamo, Gina Lollobrigida.

SYNOPSIS

Two prim English sisters, Ellen and Agnes Isit, who inherit a villa near Na-ples, move to Italy and decide to sell the property. Salvatore, the butler who has designs on the villa, begins to court Agnes. Other English people living in the district warn the girls of Salvatore's bad reputation, but Agnes is in love and will not listen to reason; she and Salvatore marry. Before long, Ellen realizes that her sister is being slowly poisoned and seeks the help of Sir Ben who forces Salvatore to confess to his crime. The two men fight and Salvatore is killed. Ellen and Ben marry and leave Naples while Agnes, believing that her husband was killed accidentally, is left alone in the villa.

Gina Lollobrigida cannot recall the rather small role played in this relatively obscure Anglo-Italian co-production. Not having seen it, but having come across an ad for it in the 1947 edition of the magazine *Fotogrammi*, in which Lollobrigida's name appears immediately after those of the lead roles, I must assume that she was more than just an extra. She probably played one of Jone Solinas' friends, and I imagine that her name was prominent for production reasons. Similarly Giuseppe Amato, whose name appears alongside that of the English director, Leslie Arliss.

L'elisir d'amore
(Elixir of Love)

1947

Produced by Prora Film. Director: Mario Costa. Story and screenplay: Mario Costa from the opera by Donizetti. Photography: Mario Bava (b/w). Art directors: Aldo Calvo and Libero Petrassi. Choreography: Viola Heermann. Organization: Angelo Di Cosmo. Distribution: Zeus Film. Origin: Italy. Running time: 82 minutes. American title: *This Wine of Love*.

CAST

Nelly Corradi (Adina), Gino Sinimberghi (Nemorino), Tito Gobbi (Belcore), Italo Tajo (Dulcamara), Loretta Di Lelio (Giannetta), and Fiorella Carmen Forti, Flavia Grande, Gina Lollobrigida, Silvana Mangano (Four girlfriends of Adina's). The chorus of the Opera of Rome directed by Gennaro D'Angelo. The Opera of Rome Ballet Company.

As one of Adina's
girlfriends.

In love with Adina, who has set her heart on Sergeant Belcore, lovesick Nemorino turns for help to Dulcamara, who sells love potions. The potions, he finds, are too weak, so Nemorino, to earn money to buy some more, joins the army. However, he soon comes into a large inheritance. As the news spreads, the village girls, Adina's friends, begin to play up to him. Then Adina learns of the reason for Nemorino's joining the army and suddenly she realizes that she is in love with him after all. Everyone in the village thinks that it is the effect of the love potion and Dulcamara is besieged by requests! Belcore lets Adina go and the two young lovers are thus free to marry.

BACKGROUND AND REVIEWS

This is the first film in which we can be certain that Lollobrigida was given a part. In fact, she was chosen by Mario Costa to play one of the girlfriends of Adina, the heroine, played by singer Nelly Corradi. Costa made his directing debut in *La sua strada* in 1943, having had a varied career as editor, screenwriter, assistant director (to Palermi and others) and production supervisor. His other films include: *Cavalcata d'eroi* (1949) with Carla Del Poggio; *Perdonami* (1954) with Antonella Lualdi and Raf Vallone; *Gli amori di Manon Lescaut* (1955) with Miriam Bru and Franco Interlenghi, *Arrivano i dollari* (1958) with Alberto Sordi and Isa Miranda.

It was Costa who really discovered Lollobrigida, the first to believe in her talent, and he went on to make two more films with her: *Follie per l'opera* and *I pagliacci*.

The following reviews offer a better idea of the type of film this was. "...*L'elisir d'amore* (in comparison with Gallone's *Rigoletto*) is a gross blunder which, in attempting to transform a stage opera into reality, instead transforms the opera into operetta...at intervals the music and singing stop, giving way to a type of prose worthy of an amateur dramatics company and, on occasions, of a puppet show! The film is a disappointment to film, opera and operetta fans alike." Carlo A. Felice, *Film*, year X, n. 30, 26 July 1947).

"It hardly seems likely, however, that *This Wine of Love* will prove to be popular with moviegoers who have no special interest in opera, for there is nothing about the film to command attention other than the music." (Thomas M. Pryor, *The New York Times*, 19 April 1948).

Follie per l'opera

1948

Produced by Scalera-Gesi (Malenotti). Director: Mario Costa. Story: Steno and Monicelli. Screenplay: Steno, Monicelli, Giovanna Soria, Mario Costa. Photography: Mario Bava (b/w). Music: Giovanni Fusco. Conductor: Giuseppe Moretti. Origin: Italy. Running time: 94 minutes. French title: *Une nuit de folie à l'opera*. English title: *Mad About Opera*.

CAST

Aroldo Tieri (Gino), Gina Lollobrigida (Dora), Constance Dowling (Margaret), Carlo Campanini (Gino's uncle), Aldo Silvani (the Priest), Franca Marzi, Beniamino Gigli, Tito Gobbi, Gino Bechi, Tito Schipa, Maria Caniglia, Nives Poli, La Scala Ballet Company, Lamberto Picasso, Guglielmo Barnabò, Nico Pepe, Luigi Almirante, Michele Riccardini.
Note: *Follie per l'opera* was the first Italian film to be bought by and released in the USSR after the war, and Lollobrigida's first film to be shown in the United States where she was billed solely as "Lollo Brigida."

As Dora, the hero's fiancée.

Gino, an Italian journalist, is trying to raise funds to rebuild a bombed-out Italian church in London. Margaret, a secretary working at Covent Garden, who is in love with him, helps him to organize a gala evening, managing to engage some of the best-known Italian singers for the occasion. But when she realizes that Gino has taken advantage of her feelings for him and is, in fact, engaged to Dora, she does all in her power to ruin the evening. With the help of his Italian friends in London, though, Gino manages to successfully reorganize his show in an improvised theater.

BACKGROUND AND REVIEWS

The film is designed to the formula of the American musical, the only difference here being that the songs have been replaced by operatic arias. In a review of the film, the magazine *Hollywood* (year IV, n. 160, 9 October 1948) describes Gina Lollobrigida as "a very beautiful young Roman girl. She plays the candid young fiancée of the enterprising hero…nothing particularly sensational."

"Mario Costa has a knack of escaping with ironical grace from the trap of conventionalism and banality into which most directors of musicals inevitably fall. Generally, the appearance in any film of a professional singer, whether it be Gino Bechi or Deanna Durbin, is enough to upset the logical flow of the action and the director's hand. And in *Follie per l'opera* there is not just one singer to deal with but three: Schipa, Gobbi and Bechi. An impossible situation almost, for one less skillful than Costa, who has already given an example of his talent for transferring from the stage to the screen, when he filmed the entire score of Donizetti's *L'elisir d'amore…*" (Arnaldo Frateili, *La Tribuna*, 5 October 1948). (Ed. Note) In her first American notice, when the film arrived in New York as *Mad About Opera* in the spring of 1950, Gina was billed both by *Variety* and *The New York Times* as Lollo Brigida (two words), in both the credits and the review itself. The *Times* looked down its nose at the film, calling it "a chunk of farce which, for silliness and overacting, has seldom been equalled hereabouts," although it had praise for offering the work of some of the top Italian singers and the La Scala Opera Company. "And in it, Lollo Brigida (sic), Constance Dowling and several reckless men strain harder, with less success, to be funnier than the Italian labor laws should allow."

An original poster. With Aroldo Tieri in the photograph, and with Constance Dowling and Tito Gobbi in the artwork (left).

I pagliacci
(Amore tragico)

1948

Produced by Itala Film. Director: Mario Costa. Story: Mario Costa and Anton Giulio Majano from the opera by Ruggero Leoncavallo. Photography: Mario Bava (b/w). Conductor: Giuseppe Morelli. Art director: Alfredo Manzi. Costumes: Nino Novarese. Editor: Otello Colangeli. Distribution: Artisti Associati. Origin: Italy. Running time: 81 minutes. English title: *Love of a Clown*. French title: *Paillasse*.

With Tito Gobbi.

CAST

Gina Lollobrigida/ voice of Onelia Fineschi (Nedda), Tito Gobbi (Tonio and Silvio), Afro Poli/ voice of Galliano Masini (Canio), Filippo Morucci/ voice of Gino Sinimberghi (Arlecchino), orchestra and Chorus of Teatro Dell' Opera of Rome.

SYNOPSIS

A company of wandering players has stopped at a small country village to give a few performances of one of their plays. Each evening Canio, Tonio, Arlecchino and Columbina enact the story of a man whose wife is cheating on him. But then one evening fiction becomes reality. Colombina has fallen in love with a local villager and has decided to run away with him. Tonio,

whose advances Colombina once refused, tells Canio what is happening. It was Canio who had found Colombina, cold and hungry and with no place to go, given her protection and married her. The next evening, during the performance Canio, as the clown, blind with jealously, stabs his wife. Her lover, seated in the audience, leaps onto the stage in an attempt to save her, but he too is killed by the clown, while panic breaks out among the spectators.

BACKGROUND AND REVIEWS

I pagliacci was made in the wake of the popularity achieved by the *Barber of Seville* and *L'elisir d'amore*, both of which were directed by Costa.

This fortunate series of film-operas lasted for a number of years and attracted such directors as Gallone, Matarazzo, Gentilomo (who made *Enrico Caruso: leggenda di una voce* with Gina Lollobrigida), Clemente Fracassi and, of course, Costa. At about the same time, there was also a series of biographical films (Verdi, Puccini etc.) and a third in which the opera was fundamental (*Follie per l'opera*, for instance).

Here, "La Lollo" plays Nedda, a dramatic role which she frankly admits having accepted only after much hesitation. The result was good, and the film was very well received abroad.

"Itala Film and Mario Costa have made *I pagliacci* for everyone. And to do so they have engaged artists of international fame, such as Tito Gobbi and Afro Poli, and a young actress named Gina Lollobrigida who only recently made her screen debut, but who already shows considerable promise." (Carlo Trabucco, *Il Popolo*, 5 April 1948).

The Paris daily *L'Autore* wrote (25 January 1950): *I pagliacci* sung by Tito Gobbi is a real treat for lovers of melodrama. But this famous baritone is also an accomplished actor, admirably supported here by Afro Poli and Gina Lollobrigida, a new star of Italian cinema, whose sensual beauty well suits the role of Nedda."

"Though it is a moot point whether she actually sings Nedda's arias, Gina Lollobrigida, who is handsomely endowed by nature, is beautiful and spirited as the faithless Nedda." (*The New York Times*, 17 April 1950).

With Aldo Poli.

"…the film offers smooth acting, excellent music and a large dose of s.a. [sex appeal] provided by its femme star, Gina Lollobrigida…[she] gives a sensual performance as the adulteress in addition to singing well." (*Variety*, 8 February 1950).

As Nedda in *I Pagliacci*.

Passaporto per l'Oriente (A Tale of Five Cities)

1949-1951

Produced by Maurice J. Wilson and Ermanno Donati for ALCE (Alleanza Cinematografica Europea) Rome and United Artists, London. Directors; Montgomery Tully, Romolo Marcellini (and Geza von Cziffra, Wolfgang Staudte, Emil E. Reinert). Story: Richard Llewellyn, Piero Tellini, Guenter Weisenborn, Jacques Companeez, Patrick Kirwan, Maurice J. Wilson. Photography: Giuseppe La Torre, Gordon Lang (b/w). Music: Francesco Mander and Hans May. Art director: Don Russell. Editor: Maurice Ruotes. Distribution: Anglo-American Film. Origin: Italy/Great Britain. French title: *L'inconnue de cinq cités*. American title: *A Tale of Five Women*. (Other suggested titles: *Storia di cinque città* and *Cinque mamme e una culla*.)

CAST

Bonar Colleano (Robert Mitchell), Barbara Kelly (Lesley McDermott), Gina Lollobrigida (Maria Severini), Marcello Mastroianni (Aldo Mazzetti), Enzo Stajola (Boy in the courtyard), Eva Bartok (Katalin Telek), Karin Himbold (Charlotte Smith), Anne Vernon (Jeannine Meunier), Raymond Bussières (Her brother), Lana Morris (Delia Morel Romanoff), Lily Kahn (Charlady), Danny Green (Levinsky), Carl Jaffe, McDonald Kork, Oleth Orr, Geoffrey Summer, Philip Leaver, Arthur Gomez, Danny Daubertson, Liliana Tellini, Annette Poivre, Lamberto Maggiorani, Charles Irwin, Vera Molnar, Craig Ivan.

SYNOPSIS

RAF pilot Robert Mitchell, an amnesiac because of an accident, finds his only link with the past in a photograph of a child and five banknotes from five different countries, on each of which is written a woman's name. With the help of a young journalist named Lesley, Robert begins searching the five capitals indicated by the banknotes for the five women and the child. In Rome, where he finds Maria, with whom he shared one fleeting hour many years before, now engaged to Aldo. He next goes to Vienna, and meets Katalin, who tells him that as a civilian he was a pilot and an artist. In Berlin, he meets Charlotte, who thanks him for having saved her from the Ges-

With Marcello Mastroianni.

tapo. In Paris, he discovers that he had a love affair with Jeannine. Finally, he reaches London, where he again is joined by Lesley, but he cannot find the girl whose name is written on the banknote. Instead, he meets Delia and suddenly his memory returns. Delia, who works in a circus, is his sister and the boy in the photograph, his nephew. Robert also remembers that the name written on the pound note is nothing more than the nickname of his major in the RAF.

BACKGROUND AND REVIEWS

As often happens with multi-part films made during that period, *Passaporto per l'Oriente* seen today is somehow intriguing. On the one hand it stars the expatriate American actor Bonar Colleano (he played opposite Lana Turner in Richard Brooks' *La fiamma e la carne* (Flame and the Flesh) made in 1954), and so well-suited to the role of a war veteran; on the other, it gives us the feeling almost that we are watching a documentary, with its fascinating glimpses of five European cities just after the war. But then again, many years have elapsed, making it easier to overlook the "stupid Atlantic propaganda and anti-Sovietism" of which the newspaper *L'Unità* wrote in a review published on 17 August 1952. The Rome episode, direction of which was refused by Rossellini, stars Gina Lollobrigida and, in only his second movie, Marcello Mastroianni, both young and pleasant to watch early in their careers. It didn't get to the United States until early 1953, and there was dismissed by the critics.

Campane a martello (Bell and Hammer)

1949

Produced by Carlo Ponti. Director: Luigi Zampa. Story and screenplay: Piero Tellini. Photography: Carlo Montuori (b/w). Music: Nino Rota. Art direction and costumes: Piero Gherardi. Editor: Eraldo Da Roma. Distribution: Lux Film. Origin: Italy/Britain. Running time: 109 minutes. French title: *Le tocsin*. English title: *O.K. Agostina*. American title: *Children of Chance*.

CAST

Gina Lollobrigida (Agostina Bortolozzi), Yvonne Sanson (Australia), Eduardo De Filippo (Don Andrea), Carlo Romano (the Maresciallo), Carlo Giustini (Marco), Clelia Matania (Bianca), Agostino Salvietti (the Mayor), Ernesto Almirante (the Landowner), Gino Saltamerenda (Ferdinando the butcher), Salvatore Arcidiacono (the Pharmacist), Ada Colangeli (Francesca), Carlo Pisacane (Filippo the altar boy), Francesco Santoro (Franco), Vittoria Febbi (Connie), Pasquale Misiano (Chauffeur).

With Yvonne Samson.

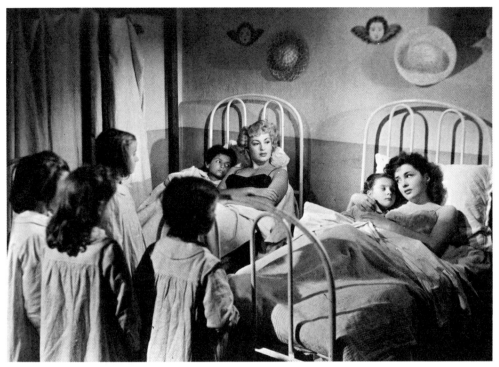

With Yvonne Samson.

Agostina is a prostitute who sends all the money she earns to her home-town priest, certain that one day she will be rich enough to be able to go back there and live a normal life. But when she and her friend Australia go one day to visit, she finds that the priest, believing that the money had been sent to him for charity, has spent all Agostina's savings to build an orphanage. Agostina demands that the money be returned to her. After much difficulty, the priest manages to scrape together the required sum, but Agostina then realizes that if she accepts it the orphanage will have to be closed. In the end, she gives the money back and returns to life in the big city.

BACKGROUND AND REVIEWS

Campane a martello is the first of three films that Gina Lollobrigida made with Luigi Zampa. The actress is at her best in *La Romana*, while Zampa, as a director, achieves his most masterful result with the superb *Processo alla città*. Though *Campane a martello* is a rather superficial film, Gina plays her role with a freshness and ease that reveal her potential talent as an actress, at least in one direction. Moreover, Agostina is a character in keeping with Italy of 1949. The scene where she returns to her home town, fearful of being recognized as a prostitute, is a situation that is fortunately a far cry from the clumsy abstractions of Lina Cavalieri's biography.

Starring with her is Yvonne Sanson, another young actress who went on to achieve success during the early '50s. (In the film, Yvonne ill-treats a little orphan girl. The Greek actress was to pay dearly for this screen gesture; in the films she was to make over the next ten years or so with Raffaello Matarazzo, children were to be for her a continual source of anguish and sorrow).

"What is this film trying to say? Even if these Jezebels do have a sense of humanity all their own. This far we agree with Zampa. But such a subject, dealt with in this way, provides us with nothing more than a study in common-place morality...All in all, the film seems more interested in showing the bosoms of Sanson and Lollobrigida than in analyzing the human condition of prostitutes and the factors that have determined this phenomenon." (Guido Aristarco, *Cinema*, year II, n. 27, 30 November 1949).

"*Campane a martello* gets off to a start that would have pleased even the author of *Maison Tellier*...but the film virtually ends after that, when the two girls, upon their arrival on the island of Ischia, discover that the local priest had thought that the money was for charity...Everything that happens from that moment on, and that is quite a lot, is nothing more than sentimental comedy, made even worse by 'the-description-of-the-typical-characters-of-the-village'....Probably, neither Zampa nor Tellini had the courage to forego the conventional 'happy ending,' to continue with the 'true story,' to show us what two prostitutes would really have done had they been 'tricked' in this manner....Imagine Maupassant's stories with endings written by De Amicis and you have an idea of the harm the cinema sometimes has to suffer." (Ennio Flaiano, *Il Mondo*, year I, n. 44, 17 December 1949).

"Beauty contest winner Gina Lollobrigida, carefully coached, shows promise in the lead." (Hawk, *Variety*, 25 January 1950).

La sposa non può attendere (The Bride Can't Wait)

1949

Produced by Baccio Bandini for Lux Film. Director: Gianni Franciolini. Story: Cesare Zavattini. Adaption: Antonio Pietrangeli. Screenplay and dialogue: Piero Tellini. Photography: Carlo Montuori (b/w). Music: Roman Vlad. Art director: Enrico Ciampi. Editor: Eraldo Da Roma. Distribution: Lux. Origin: Italy. French title: *Le mariée ne peut attendre*. Title during filming: *Anselmo ha fretta*.

CAST

Gino Cervi (Anselmo Brunelli), Gina Lollobrigida (Donata), Odile Versois (Maria, the girl who tries to commit suicide), Giacomo Furia (Giovanni), Nando Bruno (Venturi, the bride's father), Ave Ninchi (Evilina, the bride's aunt), Ada Colangeli (Sister Celeste), Gianni Baghino, Mario Meniconi, Adriano Ambrogi (the Doctor), Cesarina Rossi (Young nun), Leopoldo Valentini (Stationmaster).

Note: Gina Lollobrigida is dubbed by Dhia Cristiani.

SYNOPSIS

On his wedding day, wealthy businessman Anselmo Brunelli is driving to the town where his fiancée, Donata, lives and where they are to be married at 8:00 that morning, when he sees a young girl throw herself into the river. Anselmo saves her but then is unable to get rid of her. She is pregnant and alone and Anselmo cannot help being touched by her plight. One thing in particular strikes him: the girl has no wish to get her revenge on the man who has left her in this state. Anselmo manages to get her to a nearby convent just as labor pains begin. He then hurries to the church, but tells a lie to account for his late arrival. Still worried about the girl, he surreptitiously tries to find a midwife to send to the convent. Unfortunately, his behavior is noticed by the bride's family and a scandal breaks out. Everyone, including Donata, believes that he is the father. Cynically, they try to bribe Anselmo into keeping quiet and acting as though nothing had hap-

The poster prepared by Lux Film with the title *Anselmo ha fretta*, which was changed on the eve of its premiere.

pened. No longer a man to tolerate such a hypocritical gesture, Anselmo would rather call off the wedding, if Donata does not believe him. But she does, and their life together can begin with no shadow of suspicion to cloud it.

BACKGROUND AND REVIEWS

La sposa non può attendere is above all a story by Zavattini, in the same style as his *Quattro passi fra le nuvole* and *Prima Comunione*, both directed by Blasetti. It has the atmosphere of the former and the frenetic rhythm of the latter, and like the latter it is a moral journey, at the end of which our hero is another man.

But Franciolini's film is less incisive, events and characters being far too vaguely set in their environment. Especially during a period in which such directors as Rossellini, De Sica and Visconti were also working. If we even consider *Prima Comunione*—apart from the more obvious differences between Blasetti and Franciolini—the film's most convincing aspect is the egotistical and indifferent Rome in which Aldo Fabrizi roams.

Actors are good, especially Gina Lollobrigida, who has a freshness and spontaneity, akin to the ease and grace of many of the actresses directed by Franciolini in his more successful postwar films, like *Villa Borghese* and *Le signorine dello 04*.

The film was not embraced by the public, but it was well-received by the critics, such as Ennio Flaiano who, after having described the film as the most interesting of the year so far, adds: "The kind-hearted Anselmo...could almost be one of Labiche's characters. But unlike the bridegroom of *Cappello di paglia*, he has a humanitarian streak which torments him, throwing him into a turmoil of remorse and teaching him a sound lesson. He could have explained the misunderstanding immediately and that would have been the end of the film...But Anselmo is concerned with establishing where responsibilities lie...Besides a very convincing hero, Franciolini's film offers an excellent portrayal of village life, and yet does not make the mistake of other films in which the characters are all too conventional. Moreover, here there is a certain liveliness which lasts throughout the action..." (Ennio Flaiano, *Il Mondo*, year II, n. 42, 22 October 1950).

"Franciolini has directed this story, full of keen humor, with easy indulgence, subtly emphasizing the comical and moral aspects of the situation. Gino Cervi is excellent as the hero, as sure of himself and as convincing as ever. He is supported by Gina Lollobrigida, the gusty Nando Bruno and a pathetic Odile Versois". (Ermanno Contini, *Il Messaggero*, 2 October 1950).

Someone noticed Lollobrigida, too: "Here we are again, battling with the question of good and evil, so typical of the ultra-evangelistic Zavattini, master scriptwriter of modern Italian cinema...A nothingness created from pleasant, delicate things, some of which are witty and amusing, others less so...Gina Lollobrigida has gone another step further in her acting career. (Vice, *Il Paese*, 1 October 1950).

With an unidentified actress, Cesarina Rossi, Ada Colangeli, Ave Ninchi, Nando Bruno and an unidentified actor.

Miss Italia

1950

Produced by Carlo Ponti and Antonio
Mambretti for ATA. Director: Duilio Coletti. Story and screenplay: Fulvio Palmieri and Nino Novarese from an idea
of Alberto Lattuada. Photography:
Mario Bava (b/w). Music: Felice Mon-
tagnini. Art direction and costumes:
Piero Gherardi. Editor and assistant
director: Marino Girolami. Distribution:
Lux Film. Origin: Italy. French title: *Miss
Italie*. American title: *Miss Italy*.

CAST

Gina Lollobrigida (Lisetta Minneci),
Richard Ney (Massimo Lega), Con-
stance Dowling (Lilly), Luisa Rossi
(Gabriella), Carlo Campanini (Don Fer-
nando), Luigi Almirante (Cav. Minneci),
Umberto Melnati ("Foto-romanzo" di-
rector), Marisa Vernati (Stena Randi),
Mario Besesti (Mayor Faravelli), Mino
Doro (Guidi), Lilia Landi (Carla), Carlo
Hinterman (Livio Toschi), Mirella Uberti
(Lucia), Antonio Juva (Mario Vergani),
Barbara Leite (Nadia), Dina Perbellini
(Mrs. Favarelli), Odoardo Spadaro
(Master of ceremonies), Giuseppe
Pierozzi (Marco), Enrico Luzi (Priest),
Silvio Bagolini ("Foto-romanzo"
cameraman).

Note: Apparently, an unbilled Elsa Mor-
ante collaborated in the writing of a
story that ultimatley was not used by
Coletti. According to some, Carlo
Lizzani worked on it too.
   Gina Lollobrigida is dubbed by Dhia
Cristiani.

SYNOPSIS

   Massimo Lega, a journalist, is pre-
paring an article on the candidates of
the Miss Italy contest. The girls he
meets are from very different backgrounds, but all are propelled by a
common ambition, to win the contest
and change their way of life. Only one
of them, Lisetta, a dressmaker, did not
enter the contest of her own volition. It
was instead her father, who is certain
that his daughter will win because a
braggart named Guidi has promised
him he could sway the jury. Guidi,
however, only wants to use the man to
recover some stolen jewels.
   Once in Stresa, where the contest is
to be held, Guidi meets Lilly, one of the
competitors, whom he recognizes as a

girl he once seduced. Lilly, who has
fallen in love with Massimo, is afraid
that Guidi will try to blackmail her, but
when she discovers that Massimo is
instead in love with Lisetta, she decides to give the game away. She takes
the jewels to the police and then escapes with Guidi in a car causing it to
crash, with both being killed. Without
Lilly, Lisetta is now the favorite and is, in
fact, elected Miss Italy. As her dream
comes true, she and Massimo become
engaged.

BACKGROUND AND REVIEWS

   As can be deduced from the credits,
the film was to have been directed by
Alberto Lattuada. Just how much the
arrival on the scene of Duilio Coletti and
his team of scriptwriters contributed to
the modification of the story is difficult
to say, probably a good deal. Not that
Lattuada is a stranger to certain
topics—take *Anna* for example—but
without doubt he would have been

On the set of the film.

rhythm. Duilio Coletti has combined its various aspects with skill and shrewd direction, without probing too deeply, however, Gina Lollobrigida and Constance Dowling are the two beauties competing for the title." (Vice, *Il Messaggero*, 14 March 1951).

"...The motif was there, and it was promising—the world of the beauty queen, a world of disappointment, favoritism and vanity typical of our time. But it needed a director with greater expressive ability and poetical vision than Duilio Coletti. This film is instead banal and senseless. The two initial episodes with their political undertones are perhaps the only exceptions...Once the journalist has finished his inquiry and the action shifts to Stresa, where the contest is to take place, the story becomes a pallid excuse for a thriller, of which the less said the better. Pity." (Fabio Rinaudo, *Hollywood*, year VI, n. 238, 8 April 1950).

"Gina Lollobrigida, a comer, is slighted by script and camera as the Cinderella-type seamstress who wins the beauty title." (Hawk, *Variety*, 29 March 1950).

The New York Times (10 May 1952) found that "a whacking good story idea lost most of its merit in careless and casual hands" and that "Gina Lollobrigida and Constance Dowling, both very beautiful, give indications they could act if the director would direct them."

more perceptive of the aspects of custom and tradition that a subject like *Miss Italia* suggested. And so Italian cinema lost a golden opportunity to explore a theme that was extremely topical at that time. Coletti's *Miss Italia* is just one more of the many pedestrian films turned out by the Italian movie industry of the 1950s: pretty girls (one "good," one "bad"), an honest young man, a good-for-nothing (here Mino Doro, but more often than not Marc Lawrence), a comedian and so forth.

Moreover, the film failed to take advantage of the fact that Lollobrigida had actually taken part in a beauty contest and could, therefore, bring a touch of reality to the story. Instead, the character she plays is totally conventional.

"Thousands of young girls, every year, dream of taking part in a beauty contest and of winning the much-prized title of Miss Italia. But what are the ambitions, the true dreams of these girls?

The film has a story to tell and it has

Cuori sensa frontiere (Hearts Without Boundaries)

1950

Produced by Carlo Ponti for Lux Film. Director: Luigi Zampa. Story: Piero Tellini. Screenplay: Piero Tellini and Stefano Terra. Photography: Carlo Montuori (b/w). Music: Carlo Rustichelli. Art direction and costumes: Aldo Buzzi. Editor: Eraldo Da Roma. Distribution: Lux Film. French title: *Coeurs sans frontières?* English title: *Hearts Without Boundaries).* American title: *The White Line.* Title during filming: *Guerra o pace?* and *La linea bianca.*

CAST

Gina Lollobrigida (Donata Sebastian), Raf Vallone (Domenico), Erno Crisa (Stefano), Cesco Baseggio (Giovanni Sebastian), Enzo Staiola (Pasqualino Sebastian), Ernesto Almirante (the Grandfather), Gino Cavalieri (the Priest), Fabio Neri (Gaspare), Mario Sestan (Lampadina), Antonio Catania (Acquasanta), Giordano Cesini (Cacciavitte), Callisto Cosulich (Soviet officer), Tullio Kezich (Yugoslav lieutenant), Piero Grego (US Army sergeant), Gianni Cavalieri (Pentecoste).
Note: Uncredited Vitaliano Brancati also helped in writing the screenplay.
Gina Lollobrigida is dubbed by Lidia Simoneschi.

SYNOPSIS

The so-called "white line," the artificial boundary separating the two areas of the Venezia Guilia region, divides a small village in two. The village children often play along this line and one day they pull up one of the posts and set fire to it. Frightened that trouble might break out between the inhabitants of the two zones, one of the children tries to put the post back in its place, but in doing so is injured. The hospital is on the other side of the boundary, and the guards will not let the boy through even though his injuries are serious. Just when all seems to be lost, permission is granted to cross the "white line," a truck is even provided to rush the boy to the hospital.

BACKGROUND AND REVIEWS

In her second film with Luigi Zampa, Gina Lollobrigida plays a somewhat less colorful character than the one she played in *Campane a martello.* Here, the story counts more than the characters, and of these the children are the focus. But shabby dresses and head

With Erno Criza.

scarves can't hide Gina's beauty, and she has two men, the popular Raf Vallone and Erno Crisa, to look after her. This was former dancer Crisa's first Italian film and he is remembered primarily for his strong features. His best movies, however, were to come with De Sica's *L'oro di Napoli* (1954) and Germi's *Gelosia* (1951). Also appearing here is Enzo Staiola, the child in *Bicycle Thief*.

"This is too ambitious a film for a director such as Zampa, who has not yet reached the summit of his creative possibilities...Typical of Zampa here is his refusal to abandon, in certain situations, his favorite characterizations and banalities in the narrative which are no longer very original, and therefore have little effect. One has the impression that Zampa accepted the screenplay blindly without realizing that some of the characters are so stereotyped that they are more like puppets than flesh and blood human beings." (Fernaldo Di Giammatteo, quoted by Roberto Chiti and Giuseppe Sibilla in *Cinema*, year VIII, n. 155, 25 November 1955).

"The difficult subject matter, with its tricky political implications, is dealt with impartially and with a sense of proportion. Rarely does Zampa become banal, obvious or trite. Though he maintains his customary controversial position, which is to claim Italian rights on land so brutally divided, the film

With Raf Vallone.

favors neither friends nor enemies, in harmony with the traditional style of the man who directed *Anni difficili*. (Anonymous, *Oggi*, 26 November 1950).

The New York Times (6 December 1952) felt: "Zampa has permitted himself to be much more emotional and bombastic than is his accustomed style...Marshalling his village actors as though they were operetta choruses. As a matter of fact, Gina Lollobrigida, who plays the peasant girl, has the beauty and wistful deportment of a musical comedy star."

Vita da cani (A Dog's World)

1950

Produced by ATA, Roma. Directors: Steno and Mario Monicelli. Story and screenplay: Steno, Monicelli, Sergio Amidei, Aldo Fabrizi, Ruggero Maccari. Photography: Mario Bava (b/w). Music: Nino Rota (songs by Aldo Fabrizi, Mario Ruccione, Nino Rota). Art director: Flavio Mogherini. Editor: Mario Bonotti. Distribution: D.I. Origin: Italy. Running time: 90 minutes. French title: *Dans les coulisses*.

CAST

Aldo Fabrizi (Cavalier Nino Martoni), Gina Lollobrigida (Margherita), Delia Scala (Vera), Tamara Lees (Franca), Marcello Mastroianni (Carlo, Franca's fiancée), Nyta Dover (Lucy d'Astrid), Bruno Corelli (Ballet dancer), Furlanetto (Boselli), Gianni Barrella, Mariemma Bardi, Michele Malaspina, Tino Scotti, Pina Piovani, Lidia Alfonsi, Pasquale Misiano, Eduardo Passarelli, Enzo Maggio, Noemi Zeki, Livia Rezin, Anna Pabella, Giuseppe Angelini, Siria Vellani, Giorgina Nardini, Vittorina Benvenuti.

SYNOPSIS

Tired of her working class life in the provinces, Franca decides to try her luck in Rome. Thanks to a new-found friend, Vera, a dancer, Franca is hired by cavalier Martoni, who owns a variety troupe which unfortunately is having a hard time making ends meet. One day, the troupe is on its way to a new destination when it is joined by Margherita, a young beauty who has run away from home and immediately attracts the interest of Martoni. Vera and Franca accept the help offered by two rich businessmen, and in Franca's case the relationship ends in marriage. Vera, on the other hand, decides to go back to the troupe.

Margherita takes Franca's place and scores a real hit, which starts her on the road to big-time theatre. Meanwhile, Franca meets the hometown boy she left behind and, realizing the terrible

43

error she has made in marrying the businessman, commits suicide. Vera meets and marries a nice young man who is truly in love with her, while Margherita, much indebted to Martoni for his help, accepts an engagement with an important variety company.

BACKGROUND AND REVIEWS

In the first of the two films Lollobrigida made under the direction of Steno and Monicelli, *Vita da cani* (a film parallel, but less important than Lattuada's and Fellini's *Luci del varietà*), she plays the role of Margherita, a young provincial girl from a provincial town who joins a variety company and begins her career as a soubrette. The role is a substantial one, and offers the actress an opportunity not only to develop her character but even to sing. She shares the film, however, with two other actresses, while the place of honor goes, of course, to Aldo Fabrizi.

''Directors Monicelli and Steno... seem to have been concerned with little else other than meeting the specific artistic requirements of Aldo Fabrizi, though they have done this with a certain skill. The result is a well-made, well-balanced film with few pretensions; in other words, a film with the same limitations that characterize the humour of this popular Roman actor. Good performances are given by the other actors and actresses, among whom Gina Lollobrigida, Delia Scala and Tamara Lees...'' (Vice, *Il Paese*, 3 October 1950).

"The roving life of the small variety company, casual and precarious but at the same time friendly, is portrayed here with easy fluency through a succession of episodes, both comical and sentimental, disappointments and amusing little setbacks, colorfully animated by the presence of Aldo Fabrizi [who] has given a sense of humor to the rather cantankerous, bungling bonhomie of cavalier Nino Martoni. Gina Lollobrigida, Delia Scala and Tamara Lees are the three girls whose story is related in the film" (Ermanno Contini, *Il Messaggero*, 2 October 1950).

With Dtella Scalla and Tamara Lees.

With Della Scala.

Alina

1950

Produced by Acta Film. Director: Giorgio Pàstina. Story and screenplay: Giorgia Pàstina and Enzo Duse. Photography: Tonino Delli Colli (b/w). Music: Franco Casavola. Organization: Fabio Franchini. Origin: Italy. French title: *La fille de la nuit* or *Le fille du désir.* Title of the Italian reissue: *Alina la contrabbandiera* (1955/56).

CAST

Gina Lollobrigida (Alina), Amedeo Nazzari (Giovanni), Doris Dowling (Marie), Juan De Landa (Lucien), Otello Toso (Marco), Lauro Gazzolo (Alina's husband), Camillo Pilotto (Andrea), Nino Cavalieri (Giulio), Vittorio André, Oscar Andriani.

With Camillo Pilotto, Otello Toso and Amedeo Nazzari.

With Amedeo Nazzari.

SYNOPSIS

To make ends meet, Alina, a young woman married to an ailing older man, and two fellow villagers have become involved in smuggling that often takes them over the border into France. There they meet Giovanni, a war veteran who manages a somewhat sleazy club on behalf of Lucien, with whose singer wife Marie he is having an affair. Alina and Giovanni are attracted to one another, but Marie, out of jealousy, and Marco, a rather shady character who is friendly with Alina's husband and is determined to have the girl at all costs, stand in their way. Alina's husband and Marco come to blows, and when a fire breaks out, the old man is killed. Lucien learns of his wife's affair with Giovanni and kills her. Making a run for the Italian border, Alina and Giovanni manage to evade the police, but they are followed by Marco, who still wants Alina. The two men fight and Marco falls into a ravine. Giovanni and Alina cross the border to start a new life together.

BACKGROUND AND REVIEWS

Alina is really a sample of popular Italian cinema. So far, it has escaped reconsideration because it was directed by Pàstina rather than by Matarazzo, not that there is a great deal of difference in the long run. Lollobrigida, in the title role, puts heart and soul in vain into this improbable story. Too much character for a role dominated by the plot. The cast also included American actress Doris Dowling, sister of Constance, and best remembered for her part in *Riso amaro* (Bitter Rice). A daily newspaper and a weekly magazine reflect the general opinion at that time of this type of film. (It is obvious that the critics took for granted the unsophisticated techniques with which such films were made—techniques that have practically disappeared from routine Italian cinema. Probably for this reason, many young critics of today view these old films with renewed interest.)

"The circumstances (narrated in the film) might have given rise to an exciting and moving drama, had only the story and its psychological aspects been presented in a more credible manner. As it is, we are given situations that are pushed beyond all reality in an attempt that is detached and gratuitous. Directed by Giorgio Pàstina, the film stars Amedeo Nazzari, Gina Lollobrigida, Otello Tosi and Camillo Pilotto." (Ermanno Contini, *Il Messaggero*, 14 October 1950).

"The strip cartoon, an elementary form of graphic literature, has ruined Pàstina...In fact, both the screenplay and dialogue of *Alina* seem more suited to the comic strip than to the screen....The film has no redeeming feature and arouses little reaction, other than easy laughter, from audiences who obviously have more perception than certain directors and producers...Gina Lollobrigida's acting is almost convincing. After *La sposa non può attendere*, I wrote that she had only three expressions; in *Alina* she still has only three expressions, but she seems to be trying harder nonetheless....It is still not good enough, but she has at least made some progress." (Mario Landi, *Film d'oggi*, new series, year XIII (II), n. 8, 22 November 1950).

With Amedeo Nazzari.

47

La città si difende (The City Defends Itself)

1951

Produced by Cines. Director: Pietro Germi. Story: Federico Fellini, Tullio Pinelli, Luigi Comencini. Screenplay: Federico Fellini, Tullio Pinelli, Giuseppe Mangione, Pietro Germi. Photography: Carlo Montuori (b/w). Music: Carlo Rustichelli. Art director: Carlo Egidi. Editor: Roberto Benedetti. Distribution: Variety. Origin: Italy. Running time: 84 minutes. French title: *Traque dans la ville*. American title: *Four Ways Out*.

CAST

Gina Lollobrigida (Daniela), Renato Baldini (Paolo Leandri), Cosetta Greco (Lina Girosi), Fausto Tozzi (Luigi Girosi), Paul Müller (Guido Marchi), Patrizia Manca (Sandrina Girosi), Enzo Maggio (Alberto Tosi), Emma Baron (Alberto's mother), Tamara Lees (Woman in the portrait).
Awards: Best Italian film at the 12th Venice Film Festival, 1951.

SYNOPSIS

Four criminals rob one of the cash desks of a big soccer stadium while a match is being played. The police soon realize that the robbery is the work of amateurs. In fact, the gang includes Guido, an unsuccessful painter, Luigi, an unemployed workman, Paolo, former player, and Alberto, a hot-head who gains his inspiration from reading comic strips. At first, the four manage to elude the police, but then, one by one, they are picked up. Paolo is given away by his girlfriend, Daniela, who panics when she sees the stolen money. The painter is killed and robbed by the person who was to help him leave the country. Luigi gets involved in an argument, tries to run and, rather than be captured by the police hard on his heels, commits suicide. Alberto, his hiding place discovered, threatens to throw himself off the roof of his house, but finally is persuaded to give himself up.

BACKGROUND AND REVIEWS

Here, Gina Lollobrigida has only a

small part, that of Daniela, but her natural acting is perhaps the best of her early career. This is not surprising, considering that the director is Pietro Germi, who certainly knew how to get the best from his actors, even though this is regarded as one of his minor films. Critic Guido Aristarco remarked: "With *La città si difende*, Germi takes a definite step backwards...Having as they do little relation to time and reality, the characters in the film seem amorphous and insipid, their actions arbitrary and unjustified...even though the ending, whether intentionally or not, reminds us of Huston's *The Asphalt Jungle*. (Guido Aristarco, *Cinema*, year IV, n. 71, 1 October 1951).

Arturo Lanocita was a little more responsive toward the professionalism of Germi and his collaborators: "The film is carefully made, but carelessly conceived...The terse narrative, the elimination of all sentimental and tendential trimmings, the sober performance of actors and actresses alike, the skillful editing, bear witness to Germi's masterful directing. But there is a singular lack of inspiration, with respect to earlier films. Cameraman Carlo Montuori and actors Müller, Baldini, Maggio, Tozzi, Lollobrigida and Greco, in order of merit, do their best to assist Germi." (Arturo Lanocita, *Corriere della Sera*, 11 September 1951).

With Renato Baldini.

Enrico Caruso, leggenda di una voce

1951

Produced by Maleno Malenotti for Asso Film. Director: Giacomo Gentilomo. Story: From the novel *Neapolitanische Legende* by Frank Thiess. Screenplay: Giacomo Gentilomo, Maleno Malenotti, Fulvio Palmieri, Giovanna Soria, Piero Pierotti. Photography: Tino Santoni (b/w). Art director: Ubaldo Bonetti. Editor: Elsa Dubini. Distribution: Asso Film. Origin: Italy. Running time: 113 minutes. French title: *Caruso, la légende d'une voix.* American title: *The Young Caruso.*

CAST

Ermanno Randi (Caruso), Gina Lollobrigida (Stella), Carletto Sposito (Giovanni), Maria von Tasnady (Caruso's mother), Gaetano Verna (Caruso's father), Gino Saltamerenda (Callaro), Maurizio Di Nardo (Caruso as a boy), Ciro Scafa (Proboscide), Franca Tamantini, Lamberto Picasso, Nerio Bernardi, Elena Sangro, G. Rosmino, R. Laurienzo, R. Spiombi, and the voice of Mario Del Monaco.

Note: Of the 118 Italian films released during the 1951-52 season, this film placed nine in box office receipts.

Gina Lollobrigida is dubbed by Dhia Cristiani.

SYNOPSIS

Enrico Caruso, a poor Neapolitan boy, has a beautiful singing voice. His mother would like him to study music, but his father is against the idea. Enrico befriends an unsuccessful impresario, nicknamed Proboscide, and falls in love with Proboscide's niece, Stella. Now a grown man, Enrico once again meets Proboscide and Stella and with the impresario's help makes great progress in his singing. But when Stella marries a Sicilian nobleman, Enrico is so upset that he rejects Proboscide's guidance and joins another impresario who does little or nothing to help him. Nonetheless, in Trapani, Enrico achieves his first big success. Stella, who is in the audience, and Enrico meet one last time and vow never to see one another again.

BACKGROUND AND REVIEWS

Made the same year as MGM's more famous *The Great Caruso* with Mario Lanza, this popular film with few ambitions was Lollobrigida's biggest box office success to date. "La Lollo" plays Stella, Caruso's first love in this film tracing the famed singer's early years (unlike the Hollywood movie which takes us up to his later career). Caruso was played by Ermanno Randi, a young actor of considerable promise who died only a few months after completing the film, killed by his companion in a fit of jealousy. The affair created quite a stir and for the first time the Italian newspapers were obliged to speak openly of a homosexual relationship.

"Faced with the modest attempt by director Gentilomo, three questions spring to mind: Did the director intend to give us a film about the classics of music in the style of Carmine Gallone? Or merely an operatic concert? Or perhaps a biography of Enrico Caruso? One wonders. Starring Ermanno Randi, a young actor on his way up, Gina Lollobrigida, who stands out from the other actresses, and offering us a fair selection of operatic airs, it is not a bad film. Although, apart from a fragmentary account of the great Caruso's childhood, it would perhaps be better described as a good soundtrack, with the superb voices of soprano Maria von Tasnady and tenor Mario Del Monaco." (Bruno Brognara, *Hollywood*, year VIII, n. 336, 23 February 1952).

"Gentilomo tells his story simply, with neither flourish nor pretension...which, within limits, is perfectly acceptable. In addition, the splendid Gina Lollobrigida gives a singularly fine performance, as indeed do Ermanno Randi, Carletto Sposìto (a true revelation) etc., etc." (G.C., *Gazzetta del Popolo*, 1 November 1951).

Turning up in America in the fall of 1953 as *The Young Caruso* it received less than rave reviews from *The New York Times:* "...badly photographed, execrably edited and historically dubious...the whole affair borders on the edge of comic opera...About the only pleasant facet of the improbable production is Gina Lollobrigida and even her considerable talents are not perceptible."

Achtung! Banditi!

1951

Produced by Cooperativa Produttori Cinematografici. Director: Carlo Lizzani. Story and screenplay: Giuseppe Dagnini, Giuliani, Carlo Lizzani, Massimo Mida, Ugo Pirro, Enrico Ribulsi, Mario Socrate, Rodolfo Sonego. Photography: Gianni Di Venanzo (b/w). Music: Mario Zafred. Art director: Carlo Egidi. Editor: Enzo Alfonsi. Distribution: P.D.C. Running time: 90 minutes.

CAST

Gina Lollobrigida (Anna), Andrea Checchi (the Engineer), Lamberto Maggiorani (Marco), Vittorio Duse (Domenico), Giuseppe Taffarel (Vento), Franco Bologna (Gatto), Maria Laura Rocca (the Diplomat's lover), Giuliano Montaldo (Commissioner Lorenzo), Pietro Tordi (the Diplomat), Pietro Ferro, Bruno Berellini (Blond man).
Awards: Best director at the 7th edition of the Karlovy Vary Film Festival, 1952.

With unidentified actor.

With Andrea Checchi.

SYNOPSIS

Toward the end of the war, a group of Genoese partisans plot a raid on a local German weapons factory. The Germans discover the man who is supposed to guide them and kill him, but the partisans decide to carry on with their mission nonetheless. Dressed in civilian clothes, they enter the town unnoticed and reach the factory. At the same time, the Germans launch an attack against it with the intention of dismantling and requisitioning the machines. The workers do their best to hinder the Germans, while the partisans try to steal the weapons. But the Germans realize what is happening and take action. The day is saved by the timely arrival on the scene of the Alpini Forces.

BACKGROUND AND REVIEWS

Achtung! Banditi! was Carlo Lizzani's first feature film. Right from the years of Fascism, Lizzani had been an important film critic, who had vigorously advocated the revival of Italian cinema in the magazines *Cinema* and *Bianco e Nero*. As the subject of his first film he chose the Resistance, although by then it was 1951 and neorealism was already on the decline. Naturally, he intended to deal with the subject in a way different from that of Rossellini or of Vergano in *Il sole sorge ancora* (1946). He wanted it to be an historical film, one which portrayed the most noble page of Italy's recent history, but with neither romantic nor sentimental undertones.

Remarked Guido Aristarco (*Cinema,* year V, n. 79, 1 February 1952); "Seen from such a perspective and despite the faults of *Achtung! Banditi!*, Lizzani has given our cinema its first film about the Resistance and the first Italian historical film, after Blasetti's *1860*, and what is more, he has done it at a time when we would normally have considered a film on this subject surpassed and outdated."

The film was produced by a cooperative company, part of the money coming from voluntary contributions and with actors and technicians sharing in the costs. Gina Lollobrigida gives a fine portrayal of Anna and apart from *La città si difende*, it was the only time she appeared as a down-to-earth Italian girl tackling day-to-day problems. But Lizzani's is not an actors' movie, the real merit lies elsewhere.

Carlo Lizzani has worked a miracle in giving us Gina Lollobrigida the actress, and for this Roman "star," it is not an achievement to be taken lightly. Andrea Checchi, who plays opposite her, gives his most convincing piece of acting to date, too." (Ezio Colombo, *Hollywood*, year VIII, n. 332, 26 January 1952).

Fanfan la Tulipe
(Fanfan the Tulip)

1951

Produced by Films Ariane, Filmsonor, Giuseppe Amato. Director: Christian-Jaque. Adapted by Christian-Jaque, René Wheeler, Henri Jeanson. Screenplay: René Wheeler, René Fallet. Dialogue: Henri Jeanson. Photography: Christian Matras (b/w). Music: Georges Van Parys, Maurice Thiriet. Art Director: Robert Gys. Distribution: Dear Film. Origin: France/Italy.

CAST

Gérard Philipe (Fanfan la Tulipe), Gina Lollobrigida (Adeline), Noël Roquevert (Fortebraccio), Olivier Hussenot (Spaccamonti), Marcel Herrand (Louis XV), Jean-Marc Tennberg (Lebel), Jean Paredès (Captain de la Houlette), Nerio Bernardi (Sergeant La Franchise), Henri Rollan (the Field Marshal), Geneviève Page (Mme. de Pompadour), Sylvie Pelayo (Henriette of France), Georgette Anys (Spaccamonti's wife). Note: Gina Lollobrigida is dubbed by Adriana Parrella.

SYNOPSIS

Fanfan la Tulipe joins the army of Louis XV in order to escape from an undesirable marriage, and in the hope of fulfilling the prophesies of Adeline, the girl who loves him, who, disguised as a gypsy, has predicted a brilliant future for him. On the way to join his regiment, he saves Madame Pompadour and Henrietta, nubile daughter of Louis XV, from highwaymen. Encouraged by the two women, Fanfan steals into the royal castle in the hope of dallying with Henrietta, but he is arrested and sentenced to death. Using her charms, Adeline gains the King's favor and then asks that Fanfan be pardoned. The King agrees, but then arranges for the girl to be kidnapped and brought to the castle. Fanfan sets out to rescue her, but unwittingly crosses the enemy lines. He turns the situation at once to his advantage and captures the entire enemy General Staff. Louis XV is so grateful that he appoints Fanfan captain and consents to his marriage with Adeline.

One of the posters of the French version.

BACKGROUND AND REVIEWS

Christian-Jaque's *Fanfan la Tulipe* is the first film in which Gina Lollobrigida does not play a "victim," or a remissive character. Here, she is not only beautiful, but vivacious, captivating and impetuous. She stars opposite French matinee idol Gérard Philipe, superb in the role of Fanfan, a character made famous in a song written by Debraux in 1819.

"...a film full of spirit and movement...a delight to watch. Just imagine a bit of Rablais, a bit of Dumas and a bit of Goldoni all mixed together...Imagine the hero of a popular legend with the features of Gérard Philipe...Imagine his girlfriend with the looks of Gina Lollobrigida...a charming film altogether. (Anonymous, *Settimo Giorno*, 30 April 1952).

It is a highly enjoyable adventure film, with easy-to-follow dialogue; while

Gérard Philipe and the Italian actress Gina Lollobrigida give the story that extra touch of prestige." (Arturo Lanocita, *Corriere della Sera*, 28 April 1952).

"...it cannot have been easy to bring together on the screen Dumas, the Marx brothers, Jeanson and the distant ghost, naif and poetical, of stories about knights and damsels in distress...Besides Gérard Philipe, the cast includes a group of actors so full of enthusiasm that there were all manner of dislocated joints, sprained ankles and even broken limbs during the making of the film!" (Jean-José Richer, *Cahiers du cinéma*, year II, n. 12, May 1952).

"...played with delightful abandon by Gérard Philipe and an outstanding cast—the most conspicuously outstanding being Gina Lollobrigida, the Italian doll...most fetching as the recruiting sergeant's daughter with ample charms." (Bosley Crowther, *The New York Times*, 5 May 1953).

With Gerard Philipe.

Amor non ho...però...pergo (Love I Haven't ... But...But)

1951

Produced by France Riganti for Excelsa Film. Director: Giorgio Bianchi. Story: Giuseppe Marotta, Augusto Borselli, I. Mogherini. Screenplay: G. Marotta, A. Borselli, Franco Riganti, Vittorio Veltroni, Brancacci. Photography: Mario Bava (b/w). Art director: Mario Chiari. Editor: Adriana Novelli. Distribution: Minerva Film, Origin: Italy.

CAST

Renato Rascel (Teodoro), Gina Lollobrigida (Gina), Franca Marzi, Aroldo Tieri, Kiki Urbani, Luigi Pavese (Antonio), Nyta Dover, Guglielmo Barnabò, Carlo Ninchi, Virgilio Riento, Adriana Danieli, Galeazzo Benti.

SYNOPSIS

Teodoro, a meek and timid man, happens to be passing by when a young girl, Gina, jumps into the river. Diving in after her, Teodoro, a poor swimmer, soon finds himself in difficulty, and it is Gina herself who saves him! She tells him that she is desperate because the boy she loves is in prison accused of a crime he did not commit, and that proof of his innocence is in the hands of a criminal. Having fallen in love with Gina, Teodoro decides to help her, and after many adventures, finally catches up with the criminal and forces him to hand over the evidence. For one moment, Teodoro is tempted to destroy it so as not to lose Gina. But he overcomes the temptation, takes the evidence to the police and the innocent man is freed. Sadly, he watches Gina and her lover walk away together.

BACKGROUND AND REVIEWS

The reviews chosen to comment on this pleasant film give an idea of how little it counted in Gina Lollobrigida's screen career. In later movies, Rascel preferred partners of a more gentle kind of beauty, such as Valentina Cortese

and Marisa Pavan.

"The odd title might have given the idea that this was going to be one of those movies that Renato Rascel often uses as the backbone for a succession of clumsy sketches, dragged up from some variety show, badly filmed and singularly incoherent. However, we must give credit where credit is due, and Giorgio Bianchi has managed to draw a solid character from Rascel, placing him at the centre of a parodical story which flows smoothly and is even quite amusing at times...The photography and Gina Lollobrigida are beautiful." (Tommaso Chiaretti, *L'Unità*, 8 December 1951).

"Unlike many comic films of the current period, which are just plain vulgar, this movie, written by Marotta and Borselli, has a certain delicacy and at-tempts to combine the comical and the pathetic in a way reminiscent of Chaplin." (Fabrizio Dentice, *Giornale d'Italia*, 9 December 1951).

"The 'piccoletto' (little fellow), as Rascel likes to call himself, here plays a 'poor little fellow,' at grips with things that are too big for him, such as violence and stunningly beautiful women...Skillfully directed by Giorgio Bianchi, the film, enhanced by brief appearances of such well-known names as Ninchi, Tieri, Barnabò and others, flows at a smooth pace and raises not a few laughs from the audience. Rascel gives a good portrayal and is well supported by Luigi Pavese, in an excellent characterization of the foster brother, and the charming Gina Lollobrigida." (E.M., *Momento Sera*, 9 December 1951).

Altri Tempi (Other Times)

1952

Episode: Il processo di Frine (The Trial of Frine)

Produced by Cines. Director: Alessandro Blasetti. The episode is from a story by Edoardo Scarfoglio. Film screenplay: Alessandro Blasetti, Oreste Biancoli, Vitaliano Brancati, Gaetano Carancini, Suso Cecchi D'Amico, Alessandro Continenza, Italo Dragosei, Vinicio Marinucci, Augusto Mazzetti, Filippo Mercati, Isa Bartalini, Brunello (Gay) Rondi, Turi Vasile, G. Zucca. Photography: Carlo Montuori and Gaber Pogany. Music: Alessandro Cicognini. Art direction and costumes: Dario Cecchi and Venerio Colasanti. Editor: Mario Serandrei. Distribution: RKO. Origin: Italy. French title: *Heureuse Epoque*. American title: *Times Gone By*. Title during filming: *Zibaldone n. 1*.

CAST

Vittorio De Sica (the Lawyer), Gina Lollobrigida (Mariantonia, the accused), Giovanni Grasso, Dante Maggio, Vittorio Caprioli, Arturo Bragaglia, Carlo Mazzarella, Turi Pandolfini.
Notes: Lead roles in the other seven episodes were played by: Andrea Checchi, Alba Arnolva; Paolo Stoppa, Sergio Tofano; Amedeo Nazzari, Elisa Cegani, Roldano Lupi; Enzo Ceruscio; Rina Morelli, Barbara Florian, Vittorio Vaser and the children Maurizio Di Nardo and Geraldina Parrinello. Episodes were linked by sequences starring Aldo Fabrizi and Enzo Staiola.
Of the 146 Italian films released during the 1952-53 season, *Altri tempi* rated fifth in popular box office appeal.
The screenplay of the episode entitled *Il processo di Frine* was published in *Bianco e Nero*, year XIII, n. 5/6, May/June 1952.

SYNOPSIS

A "popolana" (woman of the people) who has killed her mother-in-law with rat poison is brought to trial and acquitted, even though she has confessed to her crime, because her skillful lawyer adroitly manages to coax her into using her natural endowments to win over judge and jury alike.

As Mariantonia in the dock.

BACKGROUND AND REVIEWS

This was the film that made Gina Lollobrigida a top movie star, perhaps in conjunction with *Fanfan la Tulipe*. However, it was in the latter film that "La Lollo" finally hit upon the role that she, and indeed many other Italian actresses were to play for many years to come: the "maggiorata fisica" (which roughly translated means "physically endowed"). This well-chosen term is derived from an episode's dialogue spoken by De Sica: "Then, on the other hand, does not the law of our land state that the mentally handicapped be acquitted? Why then should such a "physically endowed" creature as this magnificent woman beside me not be acquitted too?" Beautiful, buxom, placid, this is how "La Lollo" appears. She is on the screen for a short time only and speaks but a few lines. Her presence, however, is such that the audience's attention is attracted immediately. Not only did her fame increase tenfold with *Altri tempi*, her future in films was guaranteed. This episode also marked Vittorio De Sica's successful return to acting.

"The film is comprised of eight episodes, and eight times it gets off to a new start with no difficulty at all. Each episode has different actors, all of whom give memorable performances." (Leo Pestelli, *La Stampa*, 3 October 1952).

"The last episode of the film, *Il processo di Frine*, has just the right proportions for what it is. In fact, it is nothing more than a farce about simple country folk, but the defense of a candid, voluptuously beautiful country girl, charged with poisoning her mother-in-law, and who happens to be incapable of saying no to a man, is conducted in a vernacular vein, amid the histrionic inventions of De Sica, the lawyer. Gina Lollobrigida has only a few lines, but her physical attributes are perfectly suited to the permissive sensuality of the character she plays." (Vice, *Cinema*, year V, n. 95, 1 October 1952).

As *Times Gone By*, it was reviewed by *The New York Times*' Bosley Crowther (30 December 1953): "The vivacity of Signor de Sica as he eloquently persuades a biased court to preserve the scenic beauty of Signorina Lollobrigida is on the beam of

With Vittoro De Sica.

superbly patterned farce, and that ample young lady's smiling candor in revealing her sins and her charms is grandly droll.

Success was so great that when Blasetti decided to make *Tempi nostri* (1954), he wanted the same couple for the episode entitled *Don Corradino*, based on a story by Marotta. Wrote Blasetti (in "Trent'anni di cinema che ho vissuto," *Cinema Nuovo*, year V, n. 93, 1 November 1956): "Contrary to expectations, Gina was unable to free herself from other engagements for the ten days of filming that the episode was to take. She was busy studying French for

Siodmak and English for Huston... evidently, her international engagements were such that she could not even study a few lines of Italian for us." In the end, after some alterations had been made to the screenplay, the heroine of *Don Corradino* was played by Maria Fiore, bright young star of *Due soldi di speranza*.

Le belle della notte (The Beauty of the Night)

1952

Produced by Franco-London Film and Rizzoli Film. Director: René Clair. Story and screenplay: René Clair, Jean-Paul Grédy, P. Barillet. Photography: Armand Thirard and Robert Juillard (b/w). Music: Georges Van Parys. Art director: Léon Barsacq. Editors: Louisette Hautecoeur and Denise Natot. Distribution: Cineriz. Origin: France/Italy. Running time: 87 minutes. French title: *Les Belles de Nuit*. American title: *Beauties of the Night*.

CAST

Gérard Philipe (Claude), Martine Carol (Edmée), Gina Lollobrigida (the Cashier and Leila), Magali Vendeuil (Suzanne), Marilyn Buferd (Tobacco shop owner and Mme. Bonacieux), Raymond Bussières (Roger the Mechanic), Jean Parédès (Paul the Pharmacist), Paolo Stoppa (Opera director), Bernard La Jarrige (Leon the Policeman), Albert Michel (Postman), Henri Marchand (Henri), Raymond Cordy (Gaston), Paul Demange, Pierre Fleta, J. E. Chauffard, Bernard Dheran, Christian Chantal, Marcelle Legendre, Monique Darval, Chantal Tirède.

SYNOPSIS

Claude, a poor young musician, is suffocated by his provincial environment. Luckily, he has a vivid imagination, and every now and then escapes into a world of fantasy. The women in his dreams in different centuries have the features of the women in his everyday life, for instance Edmée, the mother of one of his pupils and cashier of the bar near home. And so he imagines that in 1900 he is challenged to a duel, in 1830 he is about to be executed, in 1789 guillotined, and the cause is always a beautiful woman! Fortunately, our hero always awakens in time and finally manages to find happiness in reality, too, such as in the smile of a pretty young neighbor.

BACKGROUND AND REVIEWS

Once again, "La Lollo" plays opposite Gérard Philipe, in this delightful film directed by René Clair. Her role here, which includes an appearance as a beautiful odalisque, is not one of her best, but it is by no means insignificant either, given the quality of the film as a whole. *Les belles de nuit* was presented at the Venice Film Festival and greeted enthusiastically, though it was judged as a momentary pause in Clair's career.

"From start to finish, Clair shows his skill as an artist of the cinema, he gives a splendid compendium of his profession and directs the camera with a bold and versatile hand [with] an array of beautiful and clever actresses: Martine Carol, Gina Lollobrigida, Magali Vendeuil, Marilyn Buferd. And the bee who draws the nectar is Gérard Philipe, whose spirited grace and aristocratic demeanor are well-known to us all." (Leo Pestelli, *La Stampa*, 11 September 1952).

"...an elegant, refined film, rich in amusing incidents and delightful little gambits, reminiscent of ballet or operetta. Not everything is brand new, on the contrary, Clair frequently repeats himself, making voluntary recourse to past gimmicks, while others are a little trite (the race in a jeep from one century to another) and not always worthy of this great director. Nonetheless, the film as a whole is pleasing and amusing, a sparklingly intelligent little comedy. To be sure, the René Clair who led us through the streets and across the roofs of Paris was of another temper; the René Clair of today is but a ghost of the old one, formal, elegant, but devoid of true expressions of the art. Shades of the prodigious ability of this famous director and his collaborators are nonetheless there..." (Tullie Kezich on *Radio Trieste*, broadcast 29 December 1952).

"The film must have served as a pretext for this famous director to reunite past experiences. The result is a sort of super-Clair, a Clair to the nth power...Giving delightful performances are Gérard Philipe, Gina Lollobrigida and Martine Carol." (Mino

Doletti, *Film d'oggi*, year XV, n. 38, 17 September 1952).

"M. Philipe as the fateful dreamer plays his role with a lively dead-pan flair, and Martine Carol, Magali Vendeuil and Gina Lollobrigida are beautiful and bright as the girls. As a matter of fact, the last, in a very scanty harem costume, which reveals that she sure isn't kidding, is a formidable attraction all alone." (Bosley Crowther, *The New York Times*, 23 March 1954).

Moglie per una notte (Bride For A Night)

1952

With Armano Francioli and Paolo Stoppa.

Produced by Rizzoli-Camerini. Director: Mario Camerini. Story and screenplay: Mario Camerini, Franco Brusati, Paolo Levi, from the play *L'ora della fantasia* (1944) by Anna Bonacci. Photography: Aldo Giordani (b/w). Music: Alessandro Cicognini. Art direction and costumes: Flavio Mogherini. Editor: Adriana Novelli. Distribution: Dear Film. Origin: Italy. Running time: 86 minutes. French title: *L'heure de la fantasie*. American title: *Wife for a Night*.

CAST

Gino Cervi (Count D'Origo), Gina Lollobrigida (Ottavia), Nadia Gray (Geraldine), Armando Francioli (Enrico Belli), Paolo Stoppa (Augusto), Galeazzo Bente (Maurizio), Paolo Panelli (Gualtieri), Eugenia Tavani (Grand Duchess), Nietta Zocchi (Yvonne), Marisa Pintus (Bettaldi), Silvio Bagolini (Silvio).

Note: The author Mario Soldati cooperated in the preparation of an earlier draft of the screenplay.

SYNOPSIS

While away on his travels, lecherous Count D'Origo meets and takes a fancy to the fascinating Geraldine, a well-known village prostitute. The mayor, Augusto, decides to take advantage of the situation in order to help his nephew, Enrico, a struggling composer. Hoping to persuade the count to sponsor Enrico, Augusto leads him to believe that Geraldine is Enrico's unglamorous wife, Ottavia, and invites him to stay at Enrico's house. Geraldine agrees to switch places with Ottavia for one night, but the plan fails when Enrico takes offense at the count's behavior and turns him out of the house. The philandering count seeks refuge in Geraldine's house and there finds the real Ottavia who has transformed herself into a ravishing beauty. He soon forgets his first desire and starts courting Ottavia, who cleverly manages to get the influential count to help in arranging a concert of her husband's music. It is an overwhelming success and Ottavia saves her reputation thanks to Geraldine, who once again resumes her libertine ways to keep the count happy.

BACKGROUND AND REVIEWS

This is our first encounter with a "plain" Gina Lollobrigida (the other being in Castellani's Mare matto). Plain, however, only to the extent that she is given a pair of glasses in the first part of the film and a dowdy hairstyle. It is difficult to understand the reason for this, unless it is to accentuate other endowments. The publicity campaign prepared by the distributors stressed the names of Gino Cervi, unforgettable protagonist of the Don Camillo films, and Gina Lollobrigida, splendid odalisque of Belle della notte...!

Worth a few brief words, too, is Anna Bonacci's comedy L'ora della fantasia ("The Dazzling Hour") from which the film is taken. In 1952, after much deliberation, and with the action transferred from England to the duchy of Parma, Camerini finally brought this version of the story to the screen. In 1964, Billy Wilder made Kiss Me, Stupid, which was basically the same story, but taking place in contemporary California. The film was intended for Marilyn Monroe, but in the end starred Kim Novak as Geraldine, the role played by Nadia Gray in the Italian version. Dean Martin (stepping in for Peter Sellers, who had suffered a heart attack) took the part played by Gino Cervi, Ray Walston that of Armando Francioli and Felicia Farr that of Gina Lollobrigida. Jeanne Moreau was instead the star of a Paris stage version.

The film was not much liked by the public, but it received some agreeable reviews from newspaper critics. "An ugly Gina Lollobrigida? Have no fear, it is only a gimmick on the part of director Camerini, and simply makes her appear more provocative...Camerini has a good deal of experience in this type of farce. And once again he has given us a film, his 33rd to be precise, full of humor and that somewhat superficial but nonetheless confident grace that always distinguishes his work." (Ugo Casiraghi, L'Unità, 18 October 1952).

"The film has much of the 'pochade' about it, but the rhythm is much gentler, possibly due to the 19th century atmosphere which Camerini adroitly, and with an odd touch of subtle irony, evokes...Good acting by Gino Cervi..., Gina Lollobrigida, whose capacity for expression grows with every new movie she makes, Nadia Gray, Paolo Stoppa and Armando Francioli." (Vice, Corriere della sera, 18 October 1952).

The New York Times (12 June 1958) called it "a frank but lightweight little sex bauble, smoothly handled and consistently amusing...Signorina Lollobrigida is, believe it or not, a virtuous plain-Jane wife (at first!) who decides not to sit idly by as the opera nears the boards. The humor comes from the ensuing confusion and crossed suspicions and, finally, from Lollobrigida's awkward attempt to play a libertine."

"Miss Lollobrigida in the voluminous gowns of a century ago is, curiously enough, a rather refreshing departure from what her couturiers have accustomed us to of late, and her performance has more conviction, perhaps because of it. (Paul V. Beckley, New York Herald Tribune, 12 June 1958.)

With Gino Cervi.

Le infedeli (The Unfaithfuls)

1953

Produced by Excelsa Film/Ponti-De Laurentiis. Directors: Steno and Monicelli. Story: Ivo Perilli. Screenplay: Ivo Perilli, Franco Brusati, Steno, Mario Monicelli. Photography: Aldo Tonti (b/w). Music: Armando Trovaioli. Art director: Flavio Mogherini. Distribution: Minerva. Origin: Italy. Running time: 97 minutes. French title: *Les infideles*.

CAST

May Britt (Liliana Rogers), Anna Maria Ferrera (Casarina), Pierre Cressoy (Osvaldo Dalprà), Gina Lollobrigida (Lulla Possenti), Irene Papas (Luisa Azzali), Marina Vlady (Marisa), Tina Lattanzi (Carla Bellaris), Giulio Calì (Investigator), Charles Fawcett (Henry Rogers), Carlo Romano (Azzali), Margherita Bagni (Marisa's mother), Milko Skofic (Guido), Tania Weber (Lulla's girlfriend), Bernardo Tafuri (Giulio Possenti), Paolo Ferrara (Police chief), Carlo Lamas (Chauffeur).

SYNOPSIS

Osvaldo Dalphrà, a young man with few scruples, is hired by the wealthy Azzali to keep an eye on the latter's wife, Luisa. Discovering that she has a lover, Osvaldo decides to blackmail her. One day, Osvaldo meets his former fiancée, Liliana Rogers, and they resume their relationship, but Osvaldo steals a necklace from her. Liliana's husband accuses the maid, Casarina, but Liliana defends her, taking the blame upon herself, and finds her a new post with the Bellaris family. Again some valuables disappear and again Casarina is accused. Arrested, she commits suicide. Liliana vows to get revenge and discovers that the second theft was the work of Lulla Possenti, who is also being blackmailed by Osvaldo because of an illicit relationship. Liliana openly accuses Osvaldo, but rather than create a scandal when the truth comes out, everybody tries to cover up the matter. Osvaldo is on the verge of going scot free through lack of evidence, but Liliana is determined to make him pay for his misdeeds.

BACKGROUND AND REVIEWS

Despite the prominence of her name in the film, Lollobrigida had only a

With Pierre Cressoy.

secondary role in *Le infedeli*. In my opinion, the movie, the last directed by Steno and Monicelli together, is over-rated, a far cry from *Guardie e ladri* or from Monicelli's later films. It is schematic and betrays its initial aim of denouncing a certain type of society, which is portrayed superficially.

Among its redeeming features: the stimulating acting of Anna Maria Ferrero and the emotional range of May Britt, the true heroine of the story. It should be said, in all fairness, that the film was well received by the critics.

"The vain and fatuous world of the so-called high society...forms the background for this tepid and cautious portrayal by Steno and Monicelli of a story by Perilli...May Britt is pleasingly photogenic. Starring with her are Gina Lollobrigida, competent and convincing, Anna Maria Ferrero and several young foreign actresses and actors." (Vittorio Sala, *Il Popolo*, 27 February 1953).

"The main theme is intertwined with many minor episodes which tend to weigh the film down somewhat. Nonetheless, the rhythm speeds up towards the end and the story takes on a controversial tone, though its criticism of 'high society' is never blatant. The direction is adequate, the 'infedeli' (unfaithfuls) are May Britt, Gina Lollobrigida, Marina Vlady, Irene Papas, while Anna Maria Ferrera plays the innocent maid and Pierre Cressoy the lover." (Gabriella Smith, *Il Paese*, 27 February 1953).

"The most important quality of *Le infedeli* is its ability, thanks to smart direction, to capture and hold the audience's attention throughout...The heroine is May Britt, a pretty young Swedish actress of no little talent...Anna Maria Ferrera too has some dramatic moments which she handles well...Gina Lollobrigida is included in the cast more for commerical reasons than for the requirements of the script." (Osvaldo Scaccia, *Film d'oggi*, year XVI, n. 10, 11 March 1953).

"The piece has punch and bite, but remains basically hackneyed... camera work is first-class, narrative is well-handled along lines familiar from French sex films of the Fifties. Gina Lollobrigida is adequate in a tiny part." (*Monthly Film Bulletin*, April 1962).

La Provinciale (The Country Wife)

1953

Produced by Ponti-De Laurentiis. Director: Mario Soldati. Story and screenplay: Mario Soldati, Sandro De Feo, Jean Ferry, Giorgio Bassani from the novel by Alberto Moravia. Photography: G.R. Aldo and Domenico Scala (b/w). Music: Franco Mannino. Art director: Flavio Mogherini. Editor: Leo Cattozzo. Distibution: Warner Bros. Origin: Italy. Running time: 90 minutes. French title: *La charmande d'amour*. English title: *The Wayward Wife*.

CAST

Gina Lollobrigida (Gemma Foresi), Gabriele Ferzetti (Franco Vagnuzzi), Alda Mangini (Elvira Coceanu), Franco Interlenghi (Paolo Sartori), Renato Baldini (Luciano Vittoni), Nando Primavera (Gemma's mother), Marilyn Buferd (Anna Sartori), Alfredo Carpegna (Count Sartori), Barbara Berg (Vannina).
Awards: Lollobrigida won a "Grolla d'oro" at the 1953 Saint Vincent Film Festival, and Ferzetti a "Nastro d'argento."

SYNOPSIS

Gemma, a pretty young provincial girl, dreams of a marriage that will enable her to break away from the stifling environment in which she lives. She falls in love with Paolo, a wealthy young man, but just before their wedding discovers that he is in reality her half-brother. Bitterly disappointed, she agrees to marry Franco, a math teacher who rents a room in the family's house. But Franco neglects her for his studies and so Gemma seeks company elsewhere. She is befriended by a Roumanian countess, who in fact only wants to take advantage of Gemma, persuading her to accept the advances of an old friend. She then blackmails Gemma into becoming a prostitute and even moves in to Gemma's house. Gemma, meanwhile, has come to understand and appreciate her husband. Desperate to hide her situation from him she tries, unsuccessfully, to

With Gabriele Ferzetti.

force the countess out, and one evening, at dinner, Gemma grabs a knife and wounds her. Franco's eyes are opened at last and he turns the countess out of their house and forgives his wife.

BACKGROUND AND REVIEWS

Starring with Gabriele Ferzetti—for whom this was his 16th film, though only the fourth as a leading man, and the one that finally made him a "star"—and Alda Mangini, Lollobrigida here plays Gemma, a character created by Alberto Moravia that was to offer the actress one of the best opportunities of her career.

La provinciale marks Mario Soldati's return to directing films of a literary origin. It is one of those rare Italian movies—together with Claudio Gora's *Febbre di vivere* and Pellegrini's *Ombre sul Canal Grande* (and in the wake of Antonioni's *Cronaca di un amore*)—to be set in a middle class environment.

The result is an interesting assembly of bitter portraits and ambiguous relationships, which was quite unusual for that period. Lollobrigida is a long way from Gemma of the book, who is described by Moravia as being "bony and graceless." But the presence of this

star in such a cynical, troubled atmosphere, where sex causes only pain and is used to achieve selfish aims, is not without a certain significance.

La provinciale is the first film in which Gina dubs herself. This is what director Soldati said in the magazine *Europeo* of 8 March 1964.

"Both Lollobrigida and Loren have made their first films in which they dubbed their own voices throughout with my direction. Sophia, because she is an intelligent actress, or because she was advised by Ponti, or for both reasons, agreed without hesitation to my idea. She threw herself into the project in that typical way of hers, determined as always to succeed. She even imitated the Ferraro accent, while Giorgio Bassani stood beside her, indicating whether the Es and Os were open or closed. Gina, on the other hand, with her naturally cautious and diffident nature, was afraid of messing things up and of ruining a budding career. It took a great deal of persuading on my part. In the end she agreed, and did extremely well. Of course from then on, neither she nor Sophia ever made another Italian film without using their own voices. And a few years later, they even spoke in English and French."

Nearly all the critics were unanimous in their enthusiasm over Soldati's return to "serious" cinema. After having noted that "the film is marked by a cold and anonymous rigor," critic Nino Ghelli went on to say: "This coldness, emphasised by banal and superficial dialogue has, of course, affected the acting, the best performance being by Gina Lollobrigida who, although failing to make the ill-conceived character of Gemma totally convincing, has at least managed to endow her with a certain measure of coherence in one of two particularly delicate moments (the episode of the chess game in which the actress is especially convincing, and her first meeting with the professor, where her acting is sober and conscientious)." (Nino Ghelli, *Bianco a Nero*, year XIV, n. 3, March 1955).

"Soldati still has not abandoned certain habits dear to him (though this is not a criticism, as long as they do not give rise to artificial style) such as interiors full of objects, people continually reflected in mirrors; nor can he resist the temptation to arrange the characters figuratively, like fragments of a pictorial composition; to use certain noises and sounds to arouse emotion. The narrative is extremely serious, the human involvement severe, according to canons of neo-realism (though Soldati has never been part of this movement)...The actors themselves are physically suited to their parts, Ferzetti and Lollobrigida in particular (what a pity that their speech is often hesitant and sometimes even incorrect)." (Lamberto Sechi, *La Settimana Incom Illustrata*, year VI, n. 12, 21 March 1953).

"It is only right that we should acknowledge the progress made by Gina Lollobrigida; but she is still only a 'presence,' not yet a mature actress. Soldati was quite right in choosing her for this role, because her physical appeal is such as to facilitate the audience's understanding of the events that occur." (Pietro Bianchi, *Il Giorno*, 27 February 1953).

"Although it has the not inconsiderable attributes of Gina Lollobrigida in the title role, it also has the somewhat stultifying effects of English-language dubbing. And while Signorina Lollobrigida desperately enacts the pangs of conscience and heartache, it is soap opera suffering that is being purveyed...She looks pained throughout, but she also is beautiful, either dressed or otherwise." (A.H. Weiler, *The New York Times*, 11 April 1955).

With Alda Mangini

Il maestro di Don Giovanni (Crossed Swords)

1953

A Viva Films Production
Produced by J. Barrett Mahon and Vittorio Vassarotti. Directors: Milton Krims and Vittorio Vassarotti. Screenplay: Milton Krims. Photography: Jack Cardiff (Pathécolor). Art director: Arrigo Equini. Costumes: Nino Novarese. Distribution: Titanus. Running time: 86 minutes. Origin: Italy/USA. English title: *Crossed Swords*.

CAST

Errol Flynn (Renzo), Gina Lollobrigida (Francesca), Cesare Danova (Raniero), Nadia Gray (Fulvia), Paola Mori (Tomasina), Roldano Lupi (Pavoncello), Alberto Rabagliati (Gennarelli), Riccardo Rioli (Lenzi), Renato Chiantoni (Spiga), Piero Tordi (The Duke), Silvio Bagolini (Buio), Mimo Billi (Miele).

SYNOPSIS

Renzo, a young nobleman of the Duchy of Sidona, returns with his friend Raniero to their native town following a long voyage. During their absence, the astute Pavoncello has been tyring to force through a law that all the young men are to marry by 20. The purpose: to increase the birthrate and consequently the military strength of the Duchy. With the arrival in town of the two friends, the decision is postponed, much to the resentment of Pavoncello. In the meantime, Renzo meets Raniero's fiery sister, Francesca, whose lady-in-waiting, Fulvia, advises her not to take Renzo seriously, as he has the reputation of being a Don Juan. Pavoncello finally manages to get his law passed and the two friends—terrified by the thought of marriage—are forced to flee. But Renzo realizes that he is genuinely in love with Francesca and cannot bear to be away from her. Pavoncello, meanwhile, now shows his true colors. He plans to seize the Duchy and attempts to do away with Renzo and Raniero, heir to the throne. Outwitting the cut-throats sent out after them, the two return home, only to find that Pavoncello has imprisoned the Duke and is planning to marry Francesca, until Renzo and Raniero

force him at sword's point to change his plan. The Duke abdicates in favor of Ramiero, who in turn abdicates in favor of his sister. She and Renzo marry and together reign over Sidona.

BACKGROUND AND REVIEWS

It was Errol Flynn himself, his fame by then on the decline, who had the idea of making *Crossed Swords*, to revive his career as the screen's pre-eminent swashbuckler. Unfortunately, films of this type, when made outside

Hollywood, rarely measure up to expectations. This was Gina's first film in color and in English. The result, at least from a visual point of view, was pleasing. The American writer, George Morris, in his book *Errol Flynn* (Pyramid Books, 1975), observes that the film's only merits are Lollobrigida and Cardiff's exquisite color photography. Among the comments on this film:

"It is pointless to go into the story of this film. We have all seen it so many times before, that we know it by heart...Flynn does his best to convince the audience, and more than likely himself as well, that he is still capable of seducing swarms of pretty young girls. Consequently, there are endless close-ups of his winning smile and knowing glance. (Marino Onorati, *Film d'oggi*, year XVII, n. 46, 18 November 1954).

"Errol Flynn leaps from window to window in this amatory adventure of a high-powered lover back in medieval Italy. It's a costumed swashbuckler offering routine escapism for undiscriminating audiences. Gina Lollobrigida and an assortment of other lovelies are the chased in the 83 minutes of footage. They, and the Italian landscape, are enhanced more by Jack Cardiff's striking Pathecolor photography than by Milton Krims' screenplay and direction, which falls into a stock groove that leaves the corn in the cob more than the tongue in the cheek...Miss Lollobrigida is a fine partner for the romancing." (*Variety*, 28 July 1954).

With Errol Flynn.

With Errol Flynn and Cesare Danova.

Il tesoro dell'Africa (Beat the Devil)

1953

Produced by Santana-Romulus and Jack Clayton. Director: John Huston. Story and screenplay: John Huston, Anthony Veiller, Peter Viertel from the novel *Beat the Devil* by James Helvick. Dialogue: Truman Capote. Photography: Oswald Morris (b/w). Music: Franco Mannino. Art director: Wilfred Shingleton. Distribution in Italy: ENIC. Origin: Great Britain/USA/Italy. Running time: 100 minutes. English title: *Beat the Devil*. French title: *Plus fort que le diable*.

CAST

Humphrey Bogart (Billy Dannreuther), Jennifer Jones (Gwendolen Chelm), Gina Lollobrigida (Maria Dannreuther), Robert Morley (Petersen), Peter Lorre (O'Hara), Edward Underdown (Harry Chelm), Ivor Bernard (Major Ross), Bernard Lee (CID Inspector), Marco Tulli (Ravello), Mario Perroni (Purser), Alex Pochet (Hotel manager), Aldo Silvani (Charles), Giulio Donnini (Administrator), Saro Urzì (Captain), Juan De Landa (Chauffeur), Manual Serano (Arab officer), Mimmo Poli (Barman), Rosario Borelli, Katherine Kath.

SYNOPSIS

American fortune hunter Billy Dannreuther and his wife Maria are among a group of adventurers waiting for a tramp steamer to take them to Africa where they hope to get their hands on a uranium mine. They meet Harry, a stuffy English peer, and Gwendolen, who takes a shine to Billy. The two join the group that also includes Billy's four "business associates," and it is not long before Maria makes overtures to Harry. En route, Harry discovers the real reason for the voyage and threatens to inform the authorities, so the other members of the group lock him in his cabin. The ship later suffers serious damage and it is then the others realize that Harry is missing. They are forced to abandon ship and come ashore in Arabia. After further adventures they finally manage to return to Italy and here they learn that Harry is still alive and has a surprise of his own.

Above, with Humphrey Bogart; below, with Peter Lorre.

BACKGROUND AND REVIEWS

This unfortunate film, which virtually disappeared many years ago, is for modern critics a sort of rebus. As often happens with films that are no longer available for viewing—especially one directed by Huston (shot entirely on

Above, with Jennifer Jones and Humphrey Bogart.
Below, with Edward Underdown, Peter Lorre, Robert Morley and Marco Tulli.
Opposite, with Humphrey Bogart.

location at Ravello in Southern Italy) with a cast of big names—curiosity tends to create a kind of mythical aura around them. Many consider this Gina Lollobrigida's best, most ironic screen performance.

In the United States, part of the film's promotion included a contest: "Can you match the measurements of Lollobrigida (Italy's Marilyn Monroe)?" Accompanying the question was a likeness of her eye-catching figure.

"In *Beat the Devil*, John Huston has again created the satirical mood of *The African Queen*. This film too should be seen as a parody...It has a feeling about it reminiscent of a joke between friends, an amusing episode involving a small, select group of people...Despite Huston's skillful directing, certain situations are left up in the air, and some of the characters are portrayed superficially. But in comparison with the glossy *Moulin Rouge* [it] is a development in Huston's career, as it takes him back to his true aspirations. Excellent performances from a very mixed, yet admirably amalgamated, cast." (Anonymous, *Cinema Nuovo*, year III, n. 28, 1 February 1954).

"(While) Gina Lollobrigida is beauteous, you cannot always understand what she is saying, as she speaks in English, but it is never important. *Beat the Devil* is a kind of shell game, with the operator sometimes forgetting under which shell the beach ball is hidden...it is a pleasant novelty all the same...[Director] John Huston is in a pixie mood here...he plays games, some hilarious and some haywire." (Otis L. Guernsey Jr., *The New York Herald-Tribune,* 13 March 1954).

"A particularly roguish and conversational spoof, generally missing the book's bite, bounce and decidedly snug construction. Gina Lollobrigida is luscious and talented [but] allowing for some genuine, brazenly funny bits, the format seems brazenly piecemeal." (Howard Thompson, *The New York Times*, 13 March 1954).

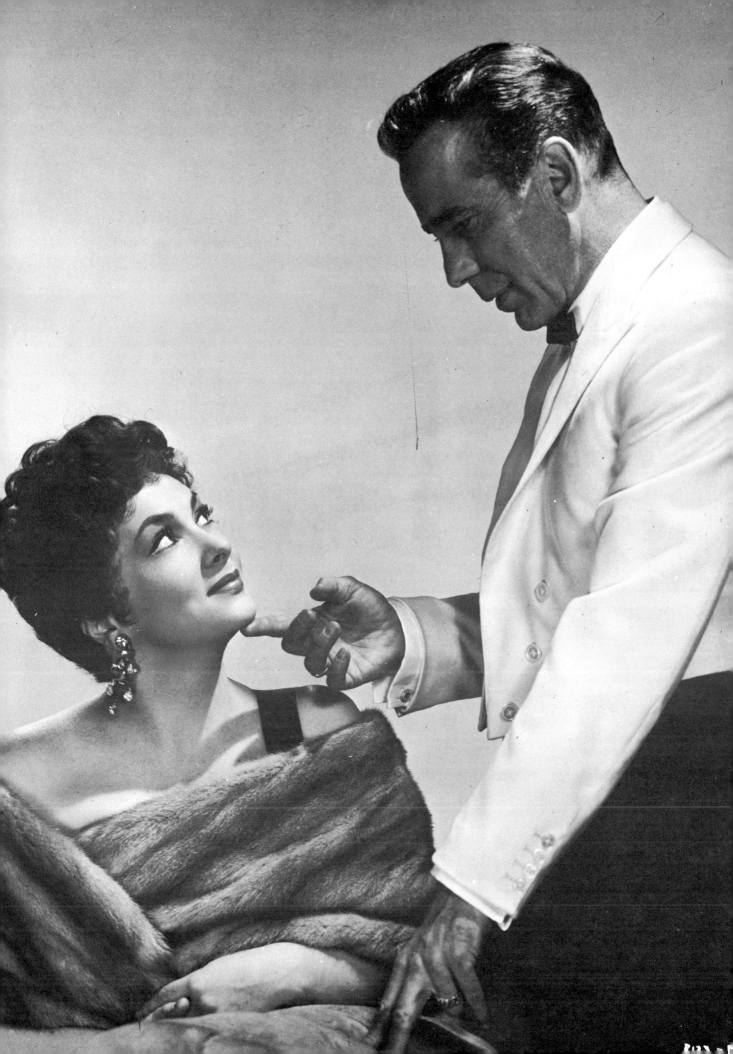

Pane, amore e fantasia (Bread, Love and Dreams)

1953

Produced by Marcello Girosi. Director: Luigi Comencini. Story and screenplay: Ettore Maria Margadonna, Luigi Comencini. Photography: Arturo Gallea (b/w). Music: Alessandro Cicognini. Art director: Gastone Medin. Editor: Mario Serandrei. Distribution: Titanus. Origin: Italy.

CAST

Vittorio De Sica (Maresciallo Carotenuto), Gina Lollobrigida (Maria De Ritis [nicknamed Pizzicarella the Bersagliera]), Roberto Risso (Pietro Stelluti), Marisa Merlini (Annarella), Tina Pica (Caramella), Virgilio Riento (don Emidio), Maria Pia Casilio (Paoletta), Memmo Carotenuto (Baiocco), Vittoria Crispo (Maria Antonia, Maria's mother), Nietta Zocchi (Country woman), Gigi Reder (Ricuccio), Fausto Guerzoni, Checco Rissone, Nino Vingelli, Alfredo Rizzo, Attilio Torelli, Ada Colangeli, Mario Meniconi.

With Virgilio Riento.

h Vittorio De Sica.

Awards: "Nastro d'argento" for Gina Lollobrigida, 1953-54 film season; "Orso d'argento" at the 1954 Berlin Film Festival; "Grolla d'oro" for Vittorio De Sica at the Saint Vincent Festival for this film and for Blasetti's *Tempi nostri*.

Note: Of the 145 Italian films released during the 1953-54 season, *Pane, amore e fantasia* was the biggest box office hit.

SYNOPSIS

Maresciallo Carotenuto reaches his new appointment, a small, isolated village perched on a hilltop. Being an incurable Don Juan, he is immediately attracted to the Bersagliera, a vivacious country girl, who has neither family nor possessions. She is in love with Stelluti, a carabiniere, who is so timid that all attempts on the girl's part to encourage him fail miserably! Carotenuto, however, has his eye on an older woman, too, Annarella, the midwife, but she is rather aloof towards him. The Bersagliera has to spend a night in the local jail, following a boisterous quarrel with a spiteful girl named Paoletta, and Carotenuto takes advantage of the situation, making a more audacious proposal to the girl. Her indignant reaction brings Carotenuto to his senses and he decides to redirect his attentions to Annarella. In the meantime, the Bersagliera has managed to overcome Stelluti's shyness and the two young people become engaged, while the relationship between Carotenuto and Annarella seems doomed to fail. Annarella is reticent and refuses to marry him, then suddenly confesses that, although unmarried, she has a son. Carotenuto forgives her, and two happy couples are thus united, though Stelluti, according to the law, must leave the village for a different post until he is old enough to marry.

REVIEWS

This was Gina Lollobrigida's first film with Luigi Comencini and perhaps her greatest success, with both critics and public alike. Some though accused it of having relinquished the spirit of neo-realism once and for all, while others acknowledged it for having brought commercial success to a branch of this movement, though this had already been the case with several other Italian films.

Its box office triumph and the distributor's shrewd exploitation of this popular series: *Pane, amore e gelosia*, *Pane, amore e...*, *Pane, amore e Andalusia*, and *Tuppe, tuppe marescià*, put to rest any further controversy. If we consider the screen career of Luigi Comencini (*Incompreso*; *Infanzia, vocazione e prime esperienze di Giacomo Casanova, veneziano*; *Pinocchio*, and the splendid *Voltati Eugenio*, which have often ranked him among Italy's most important contemporary directors), the two "*Pane, amore...*" films belong equally to writer Margadonna and the wonderful casts.

De Sica, "amiable, charming and merry" (wrote Marotta), La Lollo, a "revelation," Tina Pica (for whom the success of this film was to open the way to many more comedies), Merlini, Risso and the others are all excellent. Everybody, in fact, in the film is like those cutout figures in children's books that stand up from the pages giving an impression of reality.

"The film portrays the nicest sort of world in which to live, a world where everything turns out fine, and in the best possible way, too. A world in which all the good qualities we admire in it, the optimism emanating from it, are combined with the gaiety of a succession of extravagantly comical situations (when the maresciallo and Maria the Bersagliera fish a dress out of the water just as it is about to be carried away by the current; the maresciallo taxiing Annarella the midwife from one "birth" to another on the crossbar of his

motorized bike, whispering an eloquent and passionate avowal of eternal love in the girl's ear along the way, with quotations from Dante and other pleasantries until he loses control of the bike and the two of them end up in a heap on the grass), the wit of certain idiomatic expressions, the gusto of the many well-chosen quips, the exuberant exaggeration of certain gesticulations typical of the Abruzzi-Campania region. All this is built around the skillful acting of De Sica and Lollobrigida's naturally voluptuous beauty, in a light-hearted way, reminiscent of those sentimental comedies in vogue some years ago and for which director Mario Camerini in particular is to be remembered." (Umberto Barbaro, "Vie Nuove", year IX, n. 2, 10 January 1954).

"Signorina Lollobrigida, who is a bumptious young lady anyhow, does a grand job of playing the graceless gamine whom [Vittorio De Sica] manfully pursues. She shrills at him in derision, she mocks his graceful pleasantries and she fends off his tender advances with the most provocative twists of her shapely frame. And yet there is in her performance a suggestion of poignancy, too." (Bosley Crowther, *The New York Times,* 21 September 1954).

"Miss Lollobrigida lives up to the name of her character [Frisky] by frisking through the story in a simple frock which reveals her classic outlines. She is active as a bird, but never strident or muscular—she is beautiful." (Otis L. Guernsey, Jr., *New York Herald-Tribune,* 21 September 1954).

With Vittorio De Sica and Memmo Carotenuto.

Il grande giuoco (The Great Game)

1954

Produced by Michel Satra for Speva Film (Paris) and Rizzoli Film (Rome). Director: Robert Siodmak. Story: Jacques Feyder and Charles Spaak. Screenplay: Charles Spaak. Photography: Michel Kelber (Eastmancolor). Music: Georges Van Parys and Maurice Teiret. Art director: Leon Barsacq. Distribution: Cineriz. Origin: France/Italy. American title: *Flesh and the Woman*.

With Jean Claude Pascal.

CAST

Gina Lollobrigida (Elena e Silvia Sorrego), Jean-Claude Pascal (Pierre Martel), Arletty (Madame Blanche), Raymond Pellegrin (Mario), Peter Van Eyck (Fred), Tamerson, Odette Laure, Margo Lion, Gérard Buhr, Paul Amiet, Leila Ferida, Lila Kedrova, Umberto Melnati.

SYNOPSIS

Pierre Martel, a promising young lawyer, runs into deep trouble because of his love for beautiful, ambitious Silvia. He is obliged to flee to Algeria, where he vainly waits for the girl to join him. Signing up with the Foreign Legion, Pierre meets Elena, who bears a strong resemblance to Silvia, and falls desperately in love with her even though she is living in a whorehouse. But Pierre's misfortunes are not over. He kills a friend who tries to rape Elena and, returning to France, he again meets Silvia who, in the meantime, has married and forgotten him. Realizing that Silvia is the only one he ever really loved, he goes back to the Foreign Legion and is killed the first time his unit is sent into action.

BACKGROUND AND REVIEWS

A remake of Jacques Feyder's *Le grande jeu*, this film, directed by Robert Siomak, shows yet again that plots count little. In fact, the stories of both old and new versions are absurd and conventional, but when told by Feyder, who has style and class, they are seldom boring, so masterful is the narration. In the hands of Siodmak (who, judging by *The Spiral Staircase*, *The Killers*, and even *The Crimson Pirate*, can be an interesting director), the movie drags on arduously like some third-rate strip cartoon which, as critic Giuseppe Marotta might say, does not even have the redeeming feature of being a weekly occurrence. In other words there is no respite!

"Gina Lollobrigida warrents a comment of her own... As far as she is concerned, the matter is a little more complicated. Two characters in one. Complex sentiments, sentencious dialogue, tangled, dramatic situations. And Gina, despite the director's efforts, just cannot handle it. I would like nothing better than to be able to praise an Italian actress whose fame shows little sign of waning. But I cannot. You see, art is beauty, but beauty is not art, and this is Gina's problem." (Giuseppe Marotta, *L'Europeo*, year X, n. 40, 25 October 1954).

A Paris daily had this to say: "They decided to photograph this remake in color. A luxury that ill-suits the sordid realism of the plot...A succession of pretty images like photographs in an album...Thanks to her sincerity, Gina Lollobrigida manages to overcome the difficulty of the French language. However, strange as it may seem, the more skillful the acting, the less we are moved." (Louis Chauver, *Le Figaro*, 5 April 1954).

The film was presented at Cannes, together with *Pane, amore e fantasia*, though neither was in the award competition. For Gina it was a triumph. She signed 1610 autographs during a period of two hours in a kiosk set up specially for the occasion. A French policeman had two ribs broken while trying to keep the crowd in order.

With Arietty.

La Romana
(Woman of Rome)

1954

Produced by Excelsa-Ponti De Laurentiis. Director: Luigi Zampa. Story: from the book by Alberto Moravia. Screenplay: Luigi Zampa, Giorgio Bassani, Alberto Moravia, Ennio Flaiano. Photography: Enzo Serafin (b/w). Music: Franco Mannino. Art director: Flavio Mogherini. Editor: Eraldo Da Roma. Distribution: Minerva. Origin: Italy. Running time: 90 minutes. French title: *La belle romaine*. American title: *Woman of Rome.*

CAST

Gina Lollobrigida (Adriana), Daniel Gélin (Mino), Franco Fabrizi (Gino), Raymond Pellegrin (Astarita), Pina Piovani (Adriana's mother), Xenia Valderi (Gisella), Renato Tontini (Sonzogno), Gino Buzzanca, Mariano Bottini, Gianni Di Benedetto, Bianca Maria Cerasoli, Ada Colangeli, Vincenzo Milazzo, Riccardo Ferri, Riccardo Garrone, Alfredo De Marco, Aldo Vasco.
Note: Of the 173 Italian films released during the 1954-55 season, "La romana" rated 11th in box office receipts.

SYNOPSIS

The story takes place during Fascist times. A pretty young girl named Adriana, though encouraged by her mother to take up a life of easy morals, falls in love with Gino, a chauffeur. But Gino takes advantage of Adriana and pushes her into the arms of Astarita, an important police official. When Adriana discovers that Gino is married she has no further compunction and becomes a cynical prostitute. Among the men she meets is Mino, and it is not long before the two young people begin to feel a deep mutual affection. Mino, an anti-Fascist wanted by the police, is arrested but Adriana persuades Astarita to agree to his release. Mino believes that he has been freed due to a confession forced out of him during questioning and, fearing that he may thus have betrayed his friends, commits suicide. Adriana vows that she will never again give herself to another man but will dedicate her life to looking after the child she is carrying.

BACKGROUND AND REVIEWS

Zampa's *La romana* was presented at the Venice Film Festival the same year in which Castellani's *Romeo and Juliet* won the "Leone d'oro"—in spite of Visconti's *Senso*, a decision which even today is hard to understand. (This was also the year of: Kurosawa's *The Seven Samurai*, Mizoguchi's *L'intendente Sansho*, Fellini's *La Strada*, Kazan's *On the Waterfront*, Becker's *Grisbi*

and Hitchcock's *Rear Window*. Younger readers may well be surprised, but this was a normal line-up at a Film Festival in 1954!).

Famed novelist Italo Calvino wrote this of Lollobrigida in her starring role. (*Cinema Nuovo*, year III, n. 43, 25 September 1954):

"So far I have said nothing of Gina Lollobrigida, the very heart of the film, the reason for its being, pride and joy of the producer and of the fanatical crowd that mobbed her in their enthusiasm outside the theater. Do not think that I have left her out because I think ill of her. On the contrary, I think very well of her without, that is, wishing to idolize her. It is precisely for this reason that I shall speak of her with the seriousness and modesty that she herself has shown in playing this role. Gina Lollobrigida wants to become a good actress, a rare quality today, when abstract displays of sterile beauty and superficial improvisation are the byword. In *Pane, amore e fantasia*, she was a young shepherdess of Arcadia; here she is a real woman. Apparently, she insisted that certain episodes be included, which she felt made the character more 'human,' even though it could have altered the original Moravia character. She might be criticised for her ideas, but the reason behind them is understandable. Her almost unreal beauty seems to push her more towards conventional figures, whereas she herself seeks her protagonist within the reality of Italian society. We feel that her role as the 'Romana' has done much to help her; it is a type of 'woman of the people' she is well able to understand and define, as she is the human situation in which to place such a person: a combination of passive acceptance and acute awareness of her inevitable destiny. We cannot but encourage her in this direction."

With Raymond Pellegrin.

With Daniel Gelin.

Giulio Cesare Castello, a critic particularly observant of actors and their acting and of the "star" phenomenon in general, had this to say: "Unfortunately, Zampa here is lacking the one thing that permitted him in *Processo alla città* to evoke a living world with all its contradictions and myriad of different aspects: a good screenplay. He has made a painstaking effort to make up for this, helped by the physical presence of Gina Lollobrigida who, though not quite as convincing as in *Pane, amore e fantasia*, seems well-suited to the role of 'woman of the people.' Moreover, she shows here that she is quite capable of achieving an appreciable psychological evolution in a dramatic sense, too, despite a difficult script." (*Cinema*, year VI, n. 141, 10-25 September 1954).

"With all due respect to the lady known as Lollabrigida, *Woman of Rome* needs considerably more than Miss Gina... who carries the whole package on her beautiful shoulders [and] never looked better." (Howard Thompson, *The New York Times*, 6 November 1956)

Pane, amore e gelosia (Bread, Love and Jealousy)

1954

Produced by Marcello Girosi. Director: Lugi Comencini. Story: Ettore Maria Margadonna. Screenplay: Luigi Commencini, Ettore Maria Margadonna, Vincenzo Talarico. Photography: Carlo Montouri (b/w). Music: Alessandro Cicognini. Art director: Gastone Medin. Editor: Mario Serandrei. Distribution: Titanus. Origin: Italy. Running time: 98 minutes. American title: *Frisky*.

CAST

Vittorio De Sica (Carotenuto), Gina Lollobrigida (Maria De Ritis [nick-named the Bersagliera]), Roberta Risso (Pietro Stelluti); Marisa Merlini (Annarella), Tina Pica (Caramella), Virgilio Riento (Don Emidio), Maria Pisa Casilio, (Paoletta), Memmo Carotenuto (Baiocco), Vittoria Crispo (Maria's mother), Tecla Scarano (Trasinella), Nino Vingelli, Nico Pepe, Saro Urzi, Fausto Guerzoni, Checco Rissone, Gigi Reder, Attilio Torelli, Yvonne Sanson (the new midwife).
Notes: Of the 173 Italian films released durting the 1954-55 season, *Pane, amore e gelosia* came second as regards box office takings. Mario Camerini's *Ulisse* came first.

Eduardo and Titina De Filippo cooperated in the writing of the screenplay, but are not mentioned in the credits.

SYNOPSIS

Sagliena, the day after. Stelluti has left for his new destination while Carotenuto prepares his resignation so that he can marry Annarella, an unwed mother. But the Bersagliera goes to work in the maresciallo's house and sets the whole village gossiping. Annarella is jealous, and when Stelluti comes home on leave, he breaks off his engagement with Maria. In the meantime, the father of Annarella's child arrives in the village, determined to make amends. To get her own man back, the Bersagliera decides to join up with a group of strolling players and become a singer, but at the last minute she and Stelluti make up. Annarella marries her

With Roberto Risso.

lover, while Carotenuto seeks solace in the new midwife!

BACKGROUND AND REVIEWS

Perhaps the greatest problem facing Margadonna and his colleagues in creating the follow-up to *Pane, amore e fantasia* was that the characters were already known to the public and the element of surprise had thus been lost. In a certain sense, *Pane, amore e gelosia* is more amusing and we find that the writers have laid the greatest emphasis on the jibes and situations that aroused the most laughs in the original.

The operation was a success, but the film's inspiration was piloted, without risk, and this makes it less enjoyable even today. For the third film of the series (*Pane, amore e...*, directed by Dino Risi and starring Sophia Loren), in view of Gina's refusal to play Maria again, both Carotenuto and Caramella disappeared from the scene and new characters were introduced.

The critics, too, made similar observations. "De Sica is too much a pre-war actor to be able to liven up a plot almost as old as Italian cinema itself, however up-dated and, to use a rather ambiguous term, "neo-realist" it professes to be…'La Bersagliera,' and it can be seen more clearly here, is not a dialectical character, but rather a lower middle class girl acting a charity play before a group of friends who already know the story off by heart… Despite all this, Gina Lollobrigida does not take the film's insubstantiality 'cum grano salis'; she summon up all her talent and gives a good, convincing piece of acting, but this only helps to emphasize the fragility of the story in general." Giuseppe Turroni, *Filmcritica*, year V, n. 45, February 1955).

"Although the originality of the earlier film is lost here, the advantages of these well-chosen characters still provide amusing enough entertainment for the spectator who does not expect too much." (Vice, *Il Paese*, 24 December 1954).

"As so often happens with sequels which have no place else to go but around in uneven circles, this reprise lacks the freshness and charm…that came with *Bread, Love and Dreams*…[Lollobrigida] still wears the same drab dress which encases the same voluptuous torso. But gall seems to have got into her veins. She has become just a bit of a snarling vixen." (Bosley Crowther, *The New York Times*, 25 October 1955).

With Roberto Risso and Vittoria Crispo.

With Robert Risso, Marisa Merlini and Vfittorio De Sica.

Opposite, with Vittorio De Sica

La donna più bella del mondo (The World's Most Beautiful Woman)

1955

Produced by Maleno Malenotti. Director: Robert Z. Leonard. Story and screenplay: Casare Cavagna, Liana Ferri, Mario Monicelli, L. Martino, Piero Pierotti, Franco Solinas, Giovanna Soria, Photography: Mario Bava (Eastmancolor). Music: Renzo Rosellini. Art Director: Alberto Boccianti. Costumes: Vittorio Nino Novarese. Settings and costumes for the choreography: Venerio Colasanti. Distribution: Ge. Se. Origin: Italy. Running time: 114 minutes. French title: *La belle des belles*. American title: *Beautiful but Dangerous*.

CAST

Gina Lollobrigida (Lina Cavalieri), Vittorio Gassman (Prince Sergio), Robert Alda (Maestro Doria), Anne Vernon (Carmela), Tamara Lees (Manolita), Gino Sinimberghi, (Silvani, a singer), Nanda Primavera (Olimpia, Lina's mother), Enzo Biliotti (Perret), Marco Tulli (judge at the duel), Rolf Tasna (Lefebre), Peter Trent (Viscount Turin), Loris Gizzi (Duval), Nico Pepe, Gianni Baghine, Valeria Fabrizi, Nicla di Bruno. Voice of Mario Del Monaco

Notes: Of the Italian films released during the 1955-56 season, *La donna più bella del mondo* was the top box office hit.

The singing voice of Vittorio Gassman is dubbed by Enrico Maria Salerno.

In the film, Gina Lollobrigida personally sings arias from Tosca.

Awards: Gina Lollobrigida was awarded a "David di Donatello."

SYNOPSIS

Lina Cavalieri, a pretty young girl from the characteristic Trastevere area of Rome, has taken her mother's place in the variety show put on by the local theatre. One evening she meets Prince Sergio Bariatine, who defends her from the attentions of a vulgar spectator. When her mother dies, the girl sells the ring, the Prince had given her and uses the money to pay for singing lessons from Meastro Doria, who falls in love with her. In Paris. she and her friend Carmela, land jobs at the Eldorado, where another girl in the show, Manolita, becomes jealous of Lina's success. The two challenge one another to a duel, the event creating such a stir that it actually helps Lina in her career. Again she meets Sergio, the man she has been unable to forget. Sergio admires her, but does not recognize her and makes a bet with his friends that she will be his. When Lina discovers the bet, she runs away grieved and hurt. Her hopes dashed, Lina rushes into the arms of Silvani, a tenor, although Maestro Doria has been making persistent proposals to her, too. But during the performance of *Tosca*, the Maestro kills his rival and Lina is, once again, left alone. While on tour in Russia, Prince Sergio again crosses her path. The two at last discover that they are in love and decide to marry.

BACKGROUND AND REVIEWS

By 1955, Gina Lollobrigida was at the height of her popularity. She could do nothing wrong, in the Italian movie world, at least. Not even Sophia Loren was able to challenge her number one position. First move: become co-producer of her own film. Second move: choose her own director. After having first considered Mario Costa, then Mario Soldati, she and Malenotti agreed on a Hollywood veteran, Robert Z. Leonard. Whether or not Leonard was the right director for a film on the life of Lina Cavalieri, is a matter of opinion. It certainly did not stop the film from being an enormous box-office hit.

"In California, *Beautiful but Dangerous* would be termed a 'Lollobrigida vehicle,' in other words, a film tailor-made for the actress. It offers her every possible occasion to present to the public the full range of her artistic talents; it even underlines the similarity between Gina's life and that of Lina Cavalieri, the character she plays. It is a monument to mediocrity. In the story, the acting, the costumes, the gimmicks, all we see is the dream of a young girl who, the evening before has seen an American musical and imagines herself to be dressed like Rita Hayworth or Lana Turner while she embraces a picture postcard of Vittorio Gassman." (Tullio Kezich, *Sipario*, year X, n.116, December 1955).

"[It] is a series of picture postcards showing Gina Lollobrigida; we can almost see her dangling (you know, in one of those books of postcards that open up like a concertina) from some newsstand, gently caressed by a June morning breeze. Well now, just what has happened to Gina? Compared with the explosive Bersagliera, she seems a bit run down to me. Not that I do not like her here; on the contrary, that shadow of corruption, that perfidious shadow as it seeks and touches her, on the one hand distorts, on the other refines, spiritulaizes and promotes her. Stop being a beautiful statute and become a beautiful living creature. Not so easy, especially with this superficial biogrpahy of Lina Cavalieri...Really Gina, this is a little more than a strip cartoon story." (Giuseppe Marotta, *L'Europea*, year XII, n. 1, 5 January 1956).

"Gina Lollobrigida, the Italian vision of loveliness whose symmetry and charms are perhaps better known to moviegoers than some other treasures of Rome, has assumed, in *Beautiful But Dangerous*, the guise of Lina Cavalieri, once called 'The Most Beautiful Woman in the World.' Only a cad or another woman would dispute Signora Lollobrigida's right to the title ...breathtaking in a variety of turn-of-the-century, revealing gowns that do nothing but enhance an obviously outstanding figure." (A.H. Weiler, *The New York Times*, 6 February 1958)

GINA LOLLOBRIGIDA in — prodotto da MALENO MALENOTTI

EASTMAN COLOR

Regia di ROBERT Z. LEONARD

LA DONNA PIÙ BELLA DEL MONDO
(Lina Cavalieri)

con VITTORIO GASSMAN · ROBERT ALDA · ANNE VERNON · TAMARA LEES e con MARIO DEL MONACO

(Trapezio)
Trapeze

1956

Produced by Hecht-Hill-Lancaster for United Artists. Director: Carol Reed. Story: Liam O'Brian from the book by Max Catte. Screenplay: James R. Webb. Photography: Robert Krasker (CinemaScope-DeLuxe Color). Music: Malcolm Arnold. Art director: Rino Mondellini. Editor: Bert Bates. Distribution: Dear-U.A. Origin: USA. American title: *Trapeze*. Running time: 106 minutes.

CAST

Burt Lancaster (Mike Ribble), Gina Lollobrigida (Lola), Tony Curtis (Tino Orsini), Katy Jurado (Rosa), Thomas Gomez (Buglione), Minor Watson (John Ringling North), Gérard Landry (Cikki), Sidney James (Snake charmer), Johnny Puleo (Max the dwarf) Gamil Batib (Paul), Pierre Tabard (Stefan), J. P. Kerrien (Otto), Les Gimma Boys.
Awards: The film was presented at the 1956 Berlin Film Festival and Burt Lancaster won the award as best male actor.

SYNOPSIS

Tino Orsini, a young acrobat, joins the circus in which Mike Ribble works. Mike too had once been a famous aerialist and had had an act with Tino's father. Tino now wants Mike to teach him the dangerous triple somersault. It has been a long time since Mike did this number, but he is tempted nonetheless, and in the end agrees to teach the young man all he knows. The two men are then joined by Lola, an ambitious young girl who is determined to be part of what is bound to be the most popular act in the show. First she tries to seduce Mike, than she becomes Tino's lover, thus creating an atmosphere of jealousy and antagonism which does little to alleviate the strain of a rigorous training schedule. At last Mike and Tino carry out the famous triple somersault without a safety net, to the enthusiastic applause of the crowd. But Mike can no longer bear the relationship with Tino and Lola and decides to leave the circus. A surprise awaits him and he finds Lola, who has been in love with him from the first, is waiting outisde. The two leave together,

With Tony Curtis.

while Tino stays behind to carry on his career alone.

BACKGROUND AND REVIEWS

With *Trapeze*, Gina Lollobrigida, now Italy's number one actress and famous everywhere, had her revenge on Hollywood and began a long series of films (including *Anna di Brooklyn* and *La legge*) which was to keep her away from the Italian cinema until 1962.

Clearly, in this phase of her career, it was not the artistic quality of the film that counted, but rather the efficiency of the product, the importance of the production, the film's selling power. In other words, her ambitions had undergone a change, and this was already evident in *La donna più bella del mondo*.

And *Trapeze*? Perhaps we should ask Burt Lancaster for an explanation rather than Carol Reed, as the operation had good enough intentions at the

outset. Here anyway is a particularly objective review.

"A 'felix culpa', or rather a director's courageous error, Carol Reed's *Trapeze* is not totally lacking in ambition and does have the odd subtlety here and there. The director of *The Third Man* has attempted to transfer the emotion of a drama of passions in the world of the equestrian circus, to a higher level. In other words, he has attempted the difficult step from brute emotion to aesthetic emotion. Too intelligent and shrewd to believe that he could ennoble the drama by merely blunting the sharp edges and muting the more strident notes. Reed has actually underlined its more detrimental aspects, laying them out during the course of the story in a geometrically correct manner, so as to leave himself enough space to develop the psychological issues and illusions dearest to him. It all comes down to being a question of the screenplay (or editing, which is virtually the same thing) as envisaged by the masters of the silent era, among whom the late E. A. Dupont, whose classic *Variety* set out to achieve the same objective, and managed to do it much better". (Umberto Barbaro, *Vie Nuove*, year XII, n. 1, 5 January 1957).

"The lady in the case is played by Gina Lollobrigida, who is a singularly unsubtle siren. I suppose her contours make this inevitable." (John McCarten. *The New Yorker*, 23 June 1956).

"Gina Lollobrigida could scarcely be described as a "gimmick"—her attractions are much too durable for that. Yet undoubtedly Sir Carol Reed's exploitation of the charms of this gorgeous Italian in spangled tights (on a trapeze or off it) helps not a little to stun the audience into acceptance of his film. Perhaps La Lollo would have been happier had she been playing in Italian, not in English, but her essential gifts are international." (*Manchester* [England] *Weekly*, 5 July 1956).

th Burt Lancaster.

Notre Dame de Paris (The Hunchback of Notre Dame)

1956

Produced by Robert and Raymond Hakim for Paris Film and Panitalia. Director: Jean Delannoy. Story and screenplay: Jean Aurenche and Jacques Prévert from the novel by Victor Hugo. Photography: Michel Kelber (CinemaScope and Eastmancolor). Music: Georges Auric. Art Director: René Renoux. Editor: Henri Taverna. Distribution: Titanus. Origin: France/Italy. Running time 110 minutes. Title of the 1962 Italian reissue: *Il gobbo della cattedrale*.

CAST

Gina Lollobrigida (Esmeralda), Anthony Quinn (Quasimodo), Jean Danet (Captain Febo), Alain Cuny (Claude Frollo), Philippe Clay (Clopin Trovillefrou), Danielle Dumont (Fleur de Lys), Robert Hirsch (Gringoire), Jean Tissier (Louis XI), Valentine Tessier (Aloyse de Gondelaurier), Jacques Hilling (Charmolue), Jacques Dufilho (Guillaume Rousseau), Robert Blin (Mathias), Boris Vian (the Cardinal), Marianne Oswald (La Falourdel), Pieral (the Dwarf), Camille Guerini (The President), Darnai (Beggar Woman), Robert Lombard (Copperole), Albert Remy (Jupiter), Hubert de Lapparent (Haraucourt), Paul Bonifas (Maitre Lecornu), Madeline Barbulee (Mme. Lecornu), Albert Michel (Night watchman), Daniel Emilfork (Andry LeRouse), Georges Douking (Hoodlum).

With Anthony Quinn.

Esmeralda the gypsy girl is lusted after by Claude Frollo, a priest who delights in the study of alchemy, and who orders the church's deformed bell-ringer Quasimodo to kidnap her. Captain Febo comes to her rescue and Esmeralda falls in love with him. In his jealousy, Frollo seeks out the two lovers and wounds Febo. Esmeralda is accused of the crime, brought to trial for witchcraft and found guilty, while Febo does nothing to save her. Quasimodo saves her from the wrath of a mob and takes her to Notre Dame, where he looks after and protects her. The king finds this situation scandalous and sends his soldiers to seize the girl, but the beggars from the Cour des Miracles march on Notre Dame. As she runs to join them, Esmeralda is killed by a soldier. Quasimodo, in his desperation, slays Frollo, goes to be by Esmeralda's body and lies down beside her to await death.

BACKGROUND AND REVIEWS

Difficult as it is to become a star, it is even harder to remain one, and at this point in Gina Lollobrigida's career, she began her search for the "right part," When she went to France to make Delannoy's new version of the Victor Hugo classic, her fame was already enormous. On one occasion when she appeared in public, she was forced to seek refuge from an over-enthusiastic crowd, and more than one hundred policemen were needed to rescue her! But was *Notre Dame de Paris* a film for Lollobrigida? Filippo Sacche (*Epoca*, year VIII, 1 April 1957), in his analysis of the "star phenomenon" and of Lollobrigida in particular, offers a negative view. "The fact that 'expert' cinema men could even for one moment have considered Gina Lollobrigida for the role of a medieval gypsy, daubing her with dark make-up and covering up the milk-white complexion that is her most attractive feature, having her appear at the fair in an enormous full-length robe which shortens her legs and what is more incredible, introducing her into the atmoshere of stodgy rhetoric and legendary tragedy, which is the last thing suited to her cordial and realistic temperament, only goes to show that 'expert' cinema men do not exist!"

Among the reviews for the film itself are these:

"Delannoy's technical ability is beyond discussion, but he seems to have an unfortunate knack of turning situations and emotions to ice.... The same can be said of the actors. Gina Lollobrigida loses her natural charm and becomes a sad, resigned Esmeralda, condemned to her fate from the very first scene, while Anthony Quinn looks more like Frankenstein than Quasimodo." (Jacques Doniol-Valcroze, *France Observateur*, 27 December 1956).

"We find little in this film to applaud. Quinn's Quasimodo is an incoherent, shuffling glob of humanity so devoid of any trace of homo sapiens breeding as to be placed beyond the reach of our emotions...we were less disappointed with Miss Lollobrigida. Actually we had expected next to nothing from her and this buxom Esmeralda did little to surprise us. Even her efforts at deep breathing seemed to lack the customery force." (*Toronto Globe-Mail, 13 November 1957*).

"This version of the Victor Hugo classic, although beautifully photographed and extravagantly produced, is ponderous, often dull, and far overlength...Miss Lollobrigida appears to be somewhat miscast as a naive gypsy girl of 15th century Paris, but occasionally displays flashes of spirit." (*Variety*, 8 November 1957).

Anna di Brooklyn (Anna of Brooklyn)

1958

Produced by Milko Skofic for Circeo Cinematografica (Rome)/Les Films Marçceau (Paris). Director: Carlo Lastricati (supervised by Vittorio De Sica). Story: Ettore Maria Margadonna and Dino Risi. Screenplay: E. M. Margadonna, Luciana Corda, Joseph Stefano. Photography: Giuseppe Rotunno (Technicolor-Technirama). Art director: Gastone Medin. Music: Alessandro Cicognine, Vittorio De Sica. Editor: Eraldo Da Roma. Distribution: RKO Radio Films. Origin: Italy/France/USA. Running time 99 minutes. American title: *Fast and Sexy*.

CAST

Gina Lollobrigida (Anna), Vittorio De Sica (Don Luigi), Dale Robertson (Raffaele), Amedeo Nazzari (Ciccone), Peppino De Fillippo (Peppino), Carla Macelloni (Rosina), Gabriella Pallotta (Mariuccia), Luigi De Filippo ("Zitto-Zitto"), Clelia Matania (Camillina), Renzo Casana (the Baron), Mario Girotti (Don Luigi's nephew), Augusta Ciolli (Aunt Carmela).
Notes: The American version, titled *Fast and Sexy*, was directed by Reginald Denham.

SYNOPSIS

Anna, a girl from the Abbuzzo region of Italy, returns to her native town from America where she has been living for many years. Rich, beautiful and recently widowed, she soon becomes the main attraction in the small community, especially when it becomes known that she hopes to marry again. She sets her sights though on Raffaele, the blacksmith, who is the only man in town to take no notice of her. One after the other, the town's dignitaries pay court to Anna, using Don Luigi the local priest, to put in a good word for them first. The priest finds himself in an embarrassing situation, because his nephew is courting Rosina, who lives in the same house as Anna. Everyone believes that Anna's continual refusals are the work of Don Luigi, and that he is trying to favor his nephew's chances.

But the truth comes out in the end. Rosina decides to wed her young man, Raffaele declares his love and marries Anna, who gives up her plans to return to America.

BACKGROUND AND REVIEWS

Nobody, as far as I know, has ever seriously posed the question as to just what "supervised by Vittorio De Sica" means. That producer Milko Skofic perhaps—and Lollobrigida—felt the need to "protect" themselves, as Carlo Lastricati was making his debut as a

director? And what exactly did they ask of De Sica? To supervise the making of the film, or merely to have his name in the credits for prestige?

Or could it mean that De Sica directed the film, but did not want his name to appear as director, given that this was a minor film, and hardly went well between *Il tetto* (1956) and *La ciociara* (1960)? A complete mystery, of which not even De Sica's monographs speak.

The latter seems to me the more likely and Gina herself confirms this, adding that she remembers the involvement of neither Lastricati nor Den-

ham. Besides, it is evident that had the film been made a few years later, De Sica would have reacted differently and agreed to his name appearing as director, as was the case with *Caccia alla volpe* and *Sette volte donna*. Moreover, it was not the first time that De Sica had worked with Lollobrigida. In a sense, he had returned to the screen a second time as an actor in *Il processo di Frine* and his greatest triumphs were the films of the *Pane, amore...*series. So why should it surprise us if they decided to make a bit of fluff like *Anna di Brooklyn*" together? It is a typical example of colonial cinema. Neo-realism for export; a knick-knack conceived in the bright Italian sun for sale abroad. It certainly damaged Gina's image in Italy, but apparently not in America, for nearly ten years later she was to star in a similar type of film, *Buona Sera, Mrs. Campbell*. In addition to veteran American cowboy star Dale Robertson, the cast included Mario Girotti, who was later to become famous in spaghetti Westerns under the name of Terence Hill.

"Vittorio DeSica is listed as 'artistic supervisor' of *Fast and Sexy...*but the film bears little resemblance to such notable neo-realistic dramas as *The Bicycle Thief* and *Shoeshine*. Instead it is in the slapstick vein of the *Bread, Love and Dreams* series...Under Reginald Denham's direction, the leading lady exposes her figure far more advantageously than her acting ability." (Eugene Archer, *The New York Times*, 6 October 1960.)

La legge (The Law)

1958

Produced by GESI Cinamatografica—Titanus (Roma)—Le group des quatres (Paris), Director: Jules Dassin. Story: From the novel by Roger Vailland. Screenplay: Jules Dassin. Dialogue: Françcccoise Giroud and Diego Fabbri. Photography: Otello Martelli (b/w). Music: Roman Vlad. Art director: Robert Giordani. Editor: Roger Dwyre. Distribution: Titanus. Origin: France/Italy. Running time: 125 minutes. French title: *La loi*. American title: *Where the Hot Wind Blows*.

CAST

Gina Lollobrigida (Marietta), Pierre Brasseur (Don Cesare), Marcello Mastroianni (the Agronomist), Melina Mercouri (Donna Lucrezia), Yves Montand (Matteo Brigante), Paolo Stoppa (Tonio), Teddy Belis (Judge Alessandro), Raf Mattioli (Francesco Brigante), Vittorio Caprioli (the Police Chief), Lydia Alfonsi (Giuseppina), Gianrico Tedeschi (Unemployed man), Nino Vingelli (Pizzaccio), Bruno Carotenuto (Balbo), Herbert Knippenberg (Swiss man), Joe Dassin (Unemployed man), Marcello Giorda (the Priest), Anna Arena (Police Chief's wife, Lucia Rivelli (Elvira), Edda Soligo (Giulia, Anna Maria Bottini (Maria), Franco Pesce.

SYNOPSIS

Matteo Brigante and Don Cesare are the barons of their village on the shores of the Adriatic, although in the latter's house, at least, it is Marietta, the servant, who holds the reins. Don Cessare is married to Lucrezia, a woman who, bored with her marriage, has fallen in love with Francesco, Matteo;s young son, with whom she plans to run away. In the meantime, Marietta, hoping to marry her agronomist boyfriend, steals some money from a tourist but is found out by Matteo, who tries to rape her. She is saved from her indiscretion by Don Cesare, who returns the money and, before he dies, names her his only heir. Matteo, having found out about his son's intentions, confronts Lucrezia, making her realize just how foolish their act would be. Lucrezia leaves Francesco and commits suicide, and Matteo, after Don Cesare's death, is left alone at the head of the community, as Marietta drives away with her husband-to-be.

BACKGROUND AND REVIEWS

Lollobrigida was teamed for the only time with the expatriate American director Jules Dassin in the period between his widely acclaimed *Rififi* and *He Who Must Die*, and with a surprisingly stellar cast. The material, though was beneath them all.

"Italian neo-realism has tempted not a few foreigners; each in his own way has adapted it to suit his own purposes, but he has at least kept to 'in loco' characters and environments. At the very most, he has introduced emigrants or persons of Italian origin. Dassin, on the other hand, has been unable to resist the temptation to depict a reality that belongs essentially to our country. The result is a typically Italian story, taken from a French novel, told by an American...Moreover, in becoming

'European,' Dassin has felt the need to become intellectual too. And so we have not only the 'pastiche' described above, but also a sort of second-hand intellectualized neo-realism. A film that is all brain-work, but which tries equally to be harsh, rough, even violent. It is hardly surprising that the outcome is exactly the opposite: smooth, polished, even honeyed. This then is the style of the film. What about the structure, one might ask? Decidedly unsteady, at times it even creaks!" (Mario Gromo, *La Stampa*, 29 March 1959).

"Dassin's film...has inherited all the faults of the novel and none of its qualities. It is shapeless, awkward and rings false, even more so than the book. Nor is it redeemed by the idea to shift the little village of Porto Manacore from Puglia in southern Italy to Corsica (perhaps so as not to hurt Italian feelings!). The camouflage is all too transparent and the result is at times comical." (Enrico Rossetti, *L'Espresso*, 12 April 1959).

"...a vigorous, graphic, flowing drama of criss-crossed lives on a craggy Sicilian island...Signorina Lollobrigida, who is barefooted as she was in some of her early films, gives her best performance in years." (Howard Thompson, *The New York Times*, 12 November 1960).

Never So Few
(Sacro e Profano)

1959

Produced by Edmund Grainger for Canterbury/MGM. Director: John Sturges. Screenplay: Millard Kaufman from the novel by Tom T. Chamales. Photography: William H. Daniels (Metrocolor-Scope). Music: Hugo Friedhofer. Art directors: Hans Peters and Addison Hehr. Costumes: Helen Rose. Editor: Ferris Webster. Distribution: MGM. Origin: USA. Running time: 124 minutes. American title: *Never So Few*. French title: *La proie des vautours*. Title of the 1964 Italian reissue: *Quattro contro la morte*.

CAST

Frank Sinatra (Capt. Tom Reynolds), Gina Lollobrigida (Carla Vesari), Peter Lawford (Capt. Gray Travis), Steve Mc-Queen (Bill Ringa), Richard Johnson (Capt. Danny De Mortimer), Paul Henreid (Nikko Regas), Brian Donlevy (General Sloan), Dean Jones (Sgt. Jim Norby), Charles Bronson (Sgt. John Danforth), Philip Ann (Nautaung), Robert Bray (Col. Fred Parkson), Kipp Hamilton (Margaret Fitch), John Hoyt (Colonel Reed), Whit Bissel (Capt. Alofson), Richard Lupino (Mike Island), Aki Aleong (Billingsly), Russ Elliott (Dr. Barry), Leon Lontoc (Laurel).

During a pause in production at an MGM studio.

With Frank Sinatra.

SYNOPSIS

Capt. Tom Reynolds, commander of the allied forces in Burma, meets Carla, the mistress of war profiteer Nikko Regas, while visiting Calcutta, Reynolds' advances towards her are rejected. Back in the jungle, he is wounded in action and taken to a hospital where he again meets Carla, who tells him she has left Regas. Their friendship blossoms into romance. Once back in action, Reynolds and his men get mixed up with Chinese bandits during an attack on a Japanese airfield. Going against his colonel's advice, Reynolds has the bandits shot, getting him in trouble with the high command. He is brought before the court martial but later reinstated by General Sloan. Tom and Carla meet once more before he returns to the hills with his men.

BACKGROUND AND REVIEWS

This was Gina Lollobrigida's second American film but the first all-Hollywood one. Certainly, action director John Sturges had made better movies, such as his two most famous westerns, *Gunfight at OK Corral* (1957) and *The Magnificent Seven* (1960), and the highly entertaining *The Great Escape* (1963). Here, his most negative qualities, namely psychological approximation, action at all costs, gain the upper hand.

Lollobrigida was given the classical female role of all war films, the love interest between the action sequences, dallying with Frank Sinatra when he wasn't skirmishing with the enemy. On occasions such roles have been played by lesser actresses (Nancy Olson did it very well, as did Adele Mara or Mona Freeman, and even Dorothy Malone in her early screen days), on others by

stars of international renown (such as Eleanor Parker in *Chain Lightning* and Grace Kelly in *The Bridges of Toko-Ri*). In *Never So Few*, Gina's scenes have a light-hearted tone about them and seem to be at odds with the general context of the story. For instance, her first meeting with Sinatra takes place in a night club. For a joke, he falls down right at Gina's feet, as she enters on the arm of a distinguished looking gentleman, almost a parody of Ingrid Bergman's entrance in *Casablanca*, especially as the devoted escort is the same man, Paul Henreid.

Gina gives a good performance, but she is certainly wasted here.

Never So Few went almost unnoticed in Italy, although there were such reviews as these: "The film tells a confused story of the punitive mission of a famous US Army officer against the disloyal ally, and between one battle and another, Gina Lollobrigida puts in an appearance, without arousing much enthusiasm, however." (Anonymous, *Il nuovo spettatore cinematografico*, year II, n. 10/11. April-May 1960).

"...In the career of such a master director as John Sturges, a movie like this must be considered a mishap. We can only hope it does not happen again. Frank Sinatra is an amiable, loyal braggard. Gina Lollobrigida wears some pretty clothes." (Pietro Bianchi, *Il Giorno*, 18 March 1960).

Among the reviews from the U.S. and Great Britain were these: "In the role of the South-of-Asia femme fatale who gives up a millionaire and a life of luxury and sin for the prosaic prospect of contentment as the wife of [(the Sinatra character)], Gina Lollobrigida is quite lovely, and laughably unbelievable." (*Cue*, 23 January 1960).

"Frank Sinatra is described in the film as 'The Abe Lincoln of North Burma.' Gina Lollobrigida supplies the waiting arms, and MGM has supplied some gorgeous Oriental settings. But what might have been an explosive and searching drama turns out to be just another war-adventure film." (*The Saturday Review*, 23 January 1960).

"[The film has] a wealth of themes, most of them dropped as soon as picked up, if not sooner. Luckily, Gina Lollobrigida is there to bring us back to the one-track idiocies. 'I kiss you,' she says, 'and the bells ring wildly in my temples.'" (*The London Times*, 7 February 1960).

Solomon and Sheba (Salomone e la regina di Saba)

1959

Produced by Edward Small and Ted Richmond for Theme Pictures. Director: Kilng Vidor. Story: Crane Wilbur from the Old Testament. Screenplay: Anthony Veiller, Paul Dudly, George Bruce. Photography: Freddie Young (Technicolor - Super Technirama 70 mm). Music: Mario Nascimbene. Art directors: Richard Day and Alfred Sweeney. Editor: John Ludwig. Distribution: United Artists/Dear Films. Origin: USA. Running time: 144 minutes.

CAST

Yul Brynner (Solomon), Gina Lollobrigida (Sheba), George Sanders (Adonijah), David Farrar (Pharaoh), Marisa Pavan (Abishag), John Crawford (Joab), Laurence Naismith (Hezrai), Jose Nieto (Ahob), Alejandro Rey (Siltar), Harry ANdrews (Baltor), Julio Pena (Zadok), Finlay Currie (King David), William Devlin (Nathan), Jean Anderson (Takyan), Jack Gwillim (Josiah).
Note: The role of Solomon was to have been played by Tyrone Power, who died during filming.

th Tyrone Power in a scene that had to be reshot with Yul Brynner.

Solomon is proclaimed king of Israel, succeeding his elder brother Adonijah, and it soon becomes clear that he will be an even greater ruler. His ambitions to expand his territory are viewed unfavorably by the Pharaoh, who decided to take measures to stop him and sends the Queen of Sheba to Jerusalem to seduce him. She reaches the city accompanied by a vast cortege and it is not long before she manages to complete her wily mission. God's wrath descends ultimately upon Solomon. An enormous temple collapses and his brother takes up arms against him to win back the throne. Solomon repents, defeats his brother and repudiates the Queen of Sheba, who also asks for forgiveness and leaves Jerusalem.

BACKGROUND AND REVIEWS

This trouble-ridden epic, which had to be reshot due to the untimely death of Tyrone Power, marked the great King Vidor's retirement from motion pictures. Once again, "La Lollo" appears in a role ill-fitted to her particular talents, though by no means her figure. The Queen of Sheba would have been better suited to Hedy Lamarr or even Joan Collins. Gina had the additional handicap of her own voice which, strange as it may seem, sounded unnatural beside those of the dubbers. (The same is true of her other American-made films, and of a number of other Italian actresses as well.)

"De Mille once said that it would be possible to make a film from any three

With Yul Brynner.

pages of the Bible, and with cynical sagacity, this is just what King Vidor has tried to do. Here and there, Vidor tries to shock, for instance, the orgy in front of the idols. Looking more like the "Bersagliera" than the ancestors of Menelik (according to an Ethiopian legend), 'La Lollo' has a tête-à-tête with Solomon-Brynner, for which she wears a very transparent nocturnal combinaison, destined to become part of post-war erotic iconography." (Anonymous, *Schermi*, year III, n. 20, January-February 1960).

"[The film], although long, is not as long as most spectacles, running less than two and a half hours, but its tendency to bog down in the intermediate ogling of Gina Lollobrigida makes it seem longer than it is. Sometimes she waves about in semi-transparent gauze, sometimes in an egg-shaped tent with bronze facing...unfortunately the dancing, not only of Miss Lollobrigida (I don't suppose she ever laid claim to dancing skill) but that of the mob of squirming, overcrowded extras, is awkard and visibly uncertain." (Paul V. Beckley, *New York Herald Tribune,* 26 December 1959)

"For all its Super-Technirama, its color, its stereophonic sound and its pretensions to artistry and elegance because it was photographed in Spain, this blissfully fabricated fable of the romance of an Israelite king and an Arabic queen in the Tenth Century before Christ is strictly old-fashioned Hollywood. It stems from the jewel-in the navel and the lady-in-the-bathtub school of films...as the Queen of Sheba, Gina Lollobrigida, the original Italian overstuffed star, has the physical equipment to suggest a Little Egypt type of charmer, but her way with a love-laden line or with a spontaneous show of emotion leaves something (other than the obvious) to be desired. [As Solomon] Yul Brynner is as specious as that hair they have pasted (or he has grown) on his nude noggin. Neither it nor he suit the character." (Bosley Crowther, *The New York Times*, 26 December 1959).

With George Sanders.

Go Naked in the World (Va' nuda per il mondo)

1960

Produced by Aaron Rosenberg for Arcola/MGM. Director: Ranald Mac-Dougall. Story and screenplay: Ranald MacDougall from the novel by Tom T. Chamales. Photography: Milton Krasner (Metrocolor-Cinemascope). Music: Adolph Deutsch. Art directors: George W. Davis and Edward Carfagno. Costumes: Helen Rose. Editor: John McSweeney. Distribution: MGM. Origin: USA. Running time: 103 minutes. American title: *Go Naked in the World*. French Title: *Volupté*.

nthony Franciosa.

CAST

Gina Lollobrigida (Giulietta Cameron), Anthony Franciosa (Nick Stratton), Ernest Borgnine (Pete Stratton), Luana Patten (Yvonne Stratton), Will Kuluva (Argus Diavolos), Philip Ober (Josh Kebner), John Kellogg (Cobby), Nancy R. Pollock (Mary Stratton), Tracy Roberts (Diana), Yale Wexler (Charles Stacy), Rodney Bell (Parkson), John Gallaudet (Rupert), Chet Stratton (Jack), Maggie Pierce (Girl), Bill Smith (Boy).

SYNOPSIS

Returning G. I Nick Stratton has a falling out with his wealthy father over the Italian charmer the younger man has picked up in a San Francisco bar, blind to the fact that she's a high-priced call girl. Finally learning the truth about Giulietta Cameron's past, he decides to go against his father's will anyway and marry the girl, even though he has also found out that his father was once one of her clients. In the end, Pete Stratton, afraid of losing his son's affection forever, agrees to the marriage, but it is too late. Full of remorse for the situation she has created, and realizing that Nick will always be haunted by her past, Giulietta dons virginal white and commits suicide jumping off a cliff in Acapulco.

BACKGROUND AND REVIEWS

Gina Lollobrigida goes naked in the world, wearing splendid fur coats, each worth a small fortune, and a "drop dead" wardrobe by MGM costume designer Helen Rose. This was how the film was advertised. Fur-coated prostitutes (such as Oscar-winning Elizabeth Taylor in *Butterfield 8*) were the rage in 1960, but this particular effort

was not a very happy one. You can have too much of a good thing, after all! It should be remembered that MGM, realizing they had in *Butterfield 8* a film very similar, after changes in the screenplay, to this one, gave precedence to the Taylor movie, making many cuts in Lollobrigida's film and launching it with far less publicity. Director Ranald MacDougall had been quite a successful screenwriter: *The Breaking Point* (1950), *Mildred Pierce* (1945); *The Unsuspected* (1947), all directed by Michael Curtiz. He then became a director himself, first with a number of episodes for the *Jungle Jim* television series starring Johnny Weissmuller, and then with *Bee* (1956), *The World, the Flesh and the Devil* and *The Subterraneans*.

"...The director has so much faith in his story, it is almost as though he believes that the salvation of the motion picture world depends on films such as this... The result is utter tedium, while the dialogue is among the most dull and insipid that we have heard for a long time! It goes almost without saying that the 'immorality' of the cinema is hidden above all behind strip-cartoon efforts such as we have here. Gina Lollobrigida confirms her talent as a reasonable actress." (Ettore Zocaro, *Filmcritica*, year XII, n. 110, June 1961).

"It all boils down to the story of the call girl who had the father first, then fell in love with the son who didn't know his father had been there. Out of this whirlpool of emotion there emerges a plethora of sex, as you might imagine, along with swank joints, Acapulco for a vacation, Greek family sidelights of the less-than-believable sort, and the wan, extremely-cared-for beauty of fabulous Gina Lollobrigida." (Archer Winsten, *New York Post*, 12 March 1961).

"Gina Lollobrigida, in tight, slinky gowns and red hair, is the least hard [of the cast] to take and credit because she frankly acts what she's supposed to be—unless you are absolutely dull to the offensiveness of vulgarity and dramatic nonsequiturs, you will have stopped trying to make sense of it and taken off for fresh air before it has got this far." (Bosley Crowther, *The New York Times*, 11 March 1961).

With John Kellogg, John Gallaudet and Anthony Franciosa.

GINA LOLLOBRIGIDA · ANTHONY FRANCIOSA · ERNEST BORGNINE

VA NUDA PER IL MONDO
(Go Naked in the World)

LUANA PATTEN · WILL KULUVA · PHILIP OBER · JOHN KELLOGG · NANCY R. POLLOCK · TRACEY ROBERTS · Sceneggiatura di RANALD MacDOUGALL

in una produzione ARCOLA · dal libro di TOM T. CHAMALES · CinemaScope · METROCOLOR · Diretto da RANALD MacDOUGALL · Prodotto da AARON ROSENBERG

Come September (Torna a Settembre)

1961

With Ronald Howard.

Produced by Robert Arthur for 7 Pictures Corp./Raoul Walsh Enterprises. Director: Robert Mulligan. Story and screenplay: Stanley Shapiro and Maurice Richlin. Photography: William Daniels (CinemaScope-Technicolor). Music: Hans Salter. The song "Multiplication" composed and sung by Bobby Darin. Art director: Henry Bumstead: Editor: Russell F. Shoengarth. Distribution: Universal. Origin: USA. Running time: 112 minutes. American title: *Come September*. French title: *Le rendez-vous de septembre*.

CAST

Rock Hudson (Robert Talbot), Gina Lollobrigida (Lisa Fellini), Sandra Dee (Sandy Stevens), Bobby Darin (Tony), Walter Slezak (Maurice Clavell), Brenda De Banzie (Margaret Allison), Rossana Rory (Anna), Ronald Howard (Spencer), Joel Grey (Beagle), Ronnie Haran (Sparrow), Chris Seiz (Larry), Cindy Conroy (Julia), Joan Freeman (Linda), Nancy Anderson (Patricia), Claudia Brack (Carol), Michael Eden (Ron), Anna Maestri (Marie, the Maid), Stella Vitelleschi (Teresa, the Maid), Melinda Vikotic (Melina, the Maid), Charles Fawcett (Warren), John Stacy (Douglas), Edy Nogara (Lisa's Maid), Katherine Guilford, Helen Stirling, Franco Leasi, Milko Skofic Jr.

SYNOPSIS

Robert Talbot, a rich American playboy, spends every September at his villa near Florence in the company of the beautiful Lisa Fellini. One year, he unexpectedly arrives in July only to find to his dismay that his butler, Maurice, during the eleven months of his absence, converts the villa into a hotel named "La dolce vista"! This year, six American co-eds are in residence with their chaperone, Margaret Allison. Robert wants them to find other accommodations immediately, but Lisa persuades him to let them stay on for one more night. In the meantime, four young American men have arrived on the scene and, spotting the girls, decide to set up their tent outside the hotel. Robert becomes "mother hen" to the girls when Margaret is hospitalized after slipping on a champagne cork, but ends up quarrelling with Lisa, who makes up her mind that she has had enough of a being a one-month-a-year fiancée and returns to Rome in a huff. Thanks to the wily Maurice's schemings, Robert and Lisa meet again in Rome, on the eve of her wedding to another man! At the last moment, they patch up their quarrel, Lisa gives up

With Rock Hudson.

her other fiancée, Robert his bachelorhood, while one of the students, Tony, realizes that Sandy is much more than a holiday romance and they too become engaged.

BACKGROUND AND REVIEWS

Robert Mulligan's frothy little comedy was in stark contrast to his interesting debut movie *Fear Strikes Out* (1956). In the first of her two teamings with Rock Hudson, Gina is called Lisa Fellini and Rock's villa "La dolce vista" in an amusing bit of movie homage. Of all of Lollobrigida's American-made movies, this was her biggest box-office hit).

Certainly, we are a long way from the golden age of sophisticated comedy, and the critics were aware of it.

"Made using capital frozen in Italy (Transalpine formula according to the De Gaspari-Byrnes agreements of 25 July 1944 and 13 March 1954) this movie, like all co-productions, suffers from a flagrant lack of realism, not to mention neo-realism!" (Georges Sadoul, *Les lettres françaises*).

"[Director Robert Mulligan] has got Mr. Hudson in the right spots, doing the proper, funny things, sometimes with apparent comprehension, sometimes not. But he has got Miss Lollobrigida acting a superb comedienne, making the mistress a model of dexterity and physical allure." (Bosley Crowther, *The New York Times*, 8 September 1961).

"No matter how beautiful the surroundings, for that matter how beautiful in their various ways Lollo or Rock can be, there's always the stubborn fact that when they try to be funny, they try too hard. This time each performer will have to drag in her or his own public by main force of personal illusion, aided by the beauty of Italy. This is September on a bad day." (Archer Winsten, *New York Post*, 8 September 1961).

La bellezza di Ippolita (The Beautiful Ippolita)

1962

Produced by Alfredo Bini for Arco Film/
Cineriz/Francinex and Pathé. Director:
Giancarlo Zagni. Story: From the novel
by Elio Bartolini. Screenplay: Elio Bar-
tolini, Pasquale Festa Campanile, Mas-
simo Franciosa, Giancarlo Zagni.
Photography: Aldo Scavarda (b/w). Mu-
sic: Carlo Rustichelli. Art Director: Fla-
vio Mogherini. Editor: Nino Baragli.
Distribution: Cineriz. Origin: Italy/
France. English title: *She Got What She
Asked For.*

CAST

Gina Lollobrigida (Ippolita), Enrico
Maria Salerno (Luca), Milva (Adriana),
Lars Bloch, Carlo Giuffré, Franco
Giaobini, Ariel Mannoni, Angela Por-
taluri, Franco Balducci, Renato Mam-
bor, Piero Palermini, Bruno Scipioni.
Note: Apparently, Mario Monicelli as-
sisted in the direction of the film.

SYNOPSIS

Ippelita is a vivacious blonde chorus
girl in a second-rate variety show. Fed
up with her life on the road, she decides to marry Luca, who owns a gas
station. Ippolita is genuinely in love with
her husband, but bored with her life in
the country, distracts herself by flirting
with his customers, though never actually doing anything wrong. But Luca
does not believe this and one day, to
get his revenge, he has an affair with
one of Ippolita's girlfriends, Adriana.
Learning this, Ippolita threatens to have
an affair of her own. Of course, she
never will carry out her threat—all she
really wants is Luca—but she leaves
this sword of Damocles hanging over
her husband's head just in case!. Ultimately, Luca come to appreciate his
wife and drags her upstairs to bed.
Finally, she got what she asked for—as
the English title indicates.

BACKGROUND AND REVIEWS

This film not only marked Gina
Lollobrigida's return to Italian cinema
after four Hollywood movies, but also
demonstrated her faith in a director
making his screen debut. The story is
reminiscent of Lattuada's *La cicala,*
made 18 years earlier.

Having dyed her hair blonde for the
occasion—the publicity campaign was
built around this fact—"La Lollo" was
herself in nearly every other way: impetuous, earthy, amiable, high-spirited, rebellious, etc.

Here is what Luc Moullet (future
director) had to say the day after the

film's opening at the 1962 Berlin Film
Festival:

La bellezza di Ippolita is
Lollobrigida at her best, after *La
provinciale.* Although Italian, the film is
totally amoral: he believes that she has
been unfaithful; he gets his revenge by
being unfaithful to her; she counters: I
was not really unfaithful, but you were,
so you lead the game one-nil; now I
have to get even with you. Paralyzed by
this threat, he does everything he can
to push her into evening the score as
soon as possible. The humor is coarse
and unrestrained, making amends for
the sweetness of *Pane, amore etc.....*.
Giancarlo Zagni has got off to a good
start." (Luc Moullet, *Cahiers du cin-
èma,* year XII, n. 135, September 1962).

"Totally trivial in conception, failing
even to exploit the luminous possibilities of Miss Lollobrigida's body,
this film is difficult to appraise in any
way as there is no unity of intention…an exasperating experience to
sit through." (*Monthly Film Bulletin,*
November 1963).

Venere Imperiale
(Imperial Venus)

1962

Produced by Guido Giambartolomei. Director: Jean Delannoy. Story: Renato Castellani. Screenplay: Jean Aurenche, Leo Benvenuti, Piero De Bernardi, J. Delannoy, Arlaud. Photography: Gabor Pogany (Technicolor). Music: Francesco Lavagnino. Distribution: Cineriz. Origin: Italy/France. Running time: 140 minutes.

CAST

Gina Lollobrigida (Paolina Borghese), Stephen Boyd (Jules de Canouville), Raymond Pellegrin (Napoleon Bonaparte), Gabriele Ferzetti (Fréron), Micheline Presle (Josephine), Massimo Girotti (Leclerc), Lilla Brignone (Letizia), Giulio Bosetti (Camillo Borghese), Tino Carraro (Canova), Evi Maltagliati, Tina Lattanzi, Laura Rocca, Tom Felleghi. Awards: Gina Lollobrigida was voted best actress of 1962 and awarded the "Nastro d'argento." She also won a "David di Donatello" at the IX Taormina Film Festival.

SYNOPSIS

Beautiful, captivating and dispassionate, Paolina soon learns what it means to be the sister of Napoleon Bonaparte. She is forced to give up the man she loves and is introduced into court life. Thanks to Josephine's schemings she is married to a man named Leclerc. But the marriage does little to calm her ardent spirits, and she and her husband ultimately are sent to San Domingo, away from court gossip. The tense atmosphere of the colony does not worry Paolina who continues to enjoy herself shamelessly. When an epidemic of yellow fever breaks out and she loses her husband, however, she discovers that there is also a more dignified and heroic side to her nature. She returns to Paris and marries Camillo Borghese, after which they go to live in Rome. Boredom soon sets in and so she decides to create a stir by posing nearly nude for Canova!

Returning to Paris, she meets the one true love of her life, Jules de Canouville, but their relationship is discovered and Napoleon decides to send the officer to Russia where he is killed in action at Borodino. A now desperately unhappy Paolina stays by her brother during the days leading to his downfall, the only one able to understand him.

BACKGROUND AND REVIEWS

Venere imperiale gave considerable satisfaction to Gina Lollobrigida. Initially it was to have been filmed two years earlier by Renato Castellani, but the project had failed to materialize and ended up in a court case that kept the press busy for a while. "La Lollo" had always admired Paolina, and she is quite right from her point of view. The film covers a period of time that allows for many psychological aspects to be developed; the settings are magnificent, the costumes well-chosen. Christmas-time Italian audiences flocked to see the movie and the critics were full of praise for Gina.

"Glazed with beautiful colors, overflowing with sumptuous costumes, set in magnificent villas and palaces, starring Gina Lollobrigida, an actress dear to audiences everywhere, *Venere imperiale* has all the qualities necessary to become the most elegant, delightful film of the Christmas period." (Giovanni Grazzini, *Corriere della Sera*, 24 December 1962).

"Though retaining the character of

With Gabriele Ferzetti.

an historical film, and despite certain naivetés here and there, the odd romantic undertone and the occasional lag in the action, we can appreciate Delannoy's work here for its total lack of coarseness and for its skillful use of effect." (Dario Zanelli, *Il Resto del Carlino*, 24 December 1962).

With Raymond Pellegrin.

Mare matto (Crazy Sea)

1963

Produced by Franceso Cristaldi for Lux-Vides/Les Films Ariane. Director: Renato Castellani. Story and screenplay: Renato Castellani, Leo Benvenuti, Piero De Bernardi. Photography: Toni Secchi. Music: Carlo Rustichelli. Art Director: Carlo Leva. Editor: Iolanda Benvenuti. Distribution: Lux Film—Paramount. Origin: Itlay/France. French title: *La mer à boire*.

CAST

Gina Lollobrigida (Margherita), Jean-Paul Belmondo ("il Livornese"), Tomas Milian (Efisio), Odoardo Spadaro (Drudo Parenti), Adelmo de Fraja (Boarder), Vincenzo Musolino, Piero Morgia, Anita Durante, Rossana Di Rocco, Michele Abruzzo, Dominique Boschero (whose role was cut in the editing).

SYNOPSIS

This is a story of seafaring people: among them Efisio, a penniless sailor, who takes a room in the bording house run by Margherita, an avaricious, manipulating woman; "il Livornese", a ship's captain who becomes Margherita's lover, she being attracted more by his wealth than anything else; and old Drudo, always quarreling with his family who think it is time he retired. Drudo and "il Livornese" undertake a risky voyage to Sicily in order to deliver a shipment of wine, which is lost during a storm. Upon Drudo's return, the court orders him to pay compensation for damages.

BACKGROUND AND REVIEWS

We all agree that this was a minor multi-segment film. And we are all equally agreed on Gina Lollobrigida's excellent acting. Luigi Costantini, in *La Fiera del Cinema*, remarked that the actress arrived in Venice "in grand style, locked herself in her hotel suite and dispensed her public appearances sparingly." Many people at the Festival were sure that Gina would win the award while others, such as

With Jean Paul Belmondo.

Rondi in *Il Tempo*, after the Coppa Volpi had instead been won by Delphine Seyrig for her role in Renais' *Muriel*, spoke of an oversight on the part of the jury.

"Due merit must be given to Castellani for having made a film about a world that is new and unknown to us; for having chosen as the dialogue the quick and lively Leghorn dialect, thus achieving linguistic effects that are quite original in the Italian cinema, which is still almost totally anchored to the Roman dialect; for having explored, through the cinema, a new social class, a class whose livelihood depends on the sea; for having photographed the film so beautifully; for having chosen such a talented cast...The film is marked by the caricaturing of Odoardo Spardaro, the ham-acting of Jean-Paul Belmondo and by a new-style Lollobrigida, a trifle overdone to be honest." (Stefano Roncoroni, *Film-critica*, year XIV, n. 137 September 1963).

"Renato Castellani's work has become more refined, but it isn't always polished. He is a poet of youth. Unfortunately, he has attempted here to stimulate in adults too, from the accomplished Odoardo Spadaro to the resolute Lollobrigida, that naive and disarming inspiration, that spontaneous charm typical of youth, without which his work becomes sterile calligraphy, ornate rhetoric..." (Pietro Bianchi, *Il Giorno*, 2 September 1963).

The film deals principally with Margherita (Gina Lollobrigida), a stingy old maid who falls for a young boarder (Belmondo)...Lollobrigida is good in an offbeat role; J. P. Belmondo at home in the role of the likeable never do well." (Hawk, *Variety*, 18 September 1963)

It should, in all fairness, be remembered that numerous cuts were made in Castellani's film (in part to satisfy the producers) before it actually reached the screen, and this certainly did more harm than good, especially as they concerned the film's more mythical aspect (for instance, the episode of the siren played by Dominique Boschero was cut out completely).

Woman of Straw (La donna di paglia)

1963

With Sean Connery.

Produced by Michael Relph and Basil Dearden for United Artists (Great Britain). Story: Catherine Arley from her novel *La femme de paille*. Screenplay: Robert Muller and Stanley Mann. Photography: Otto Heller (Eastmancolor). Music: Norman Percival. Production designer: Ken Adam. Editor: John B. Gutheridge. Gina Lollobrigida's clothes by Dior. Distribution: Dear. Origin: Great Britain. Running time: 117 minutes. English title: *Woman of Straw*.

CAST

Gina Lollobrigida (Maria Marcello), Sean Connery (Anthony Richmond), Ralph Richardson (Charles Richmond), Johnny Sekka (Thomas), Laurence Hardy (Baines), Danny Daniels (Fenton), Alexander Knox (Lomer), Peter Madden (Yacht captain), André Morel (Judge), Michael Goodliffe (Penfeld), Douglas Wilmer (Dr. Murray), Robert Bruce (chauffeur), Peggy Marshall (Wardress), Edward Underdown (1st executive), George Curzon (2nd executive), A.J. Brown (3rd executive).

SYNOPSIS

When Anthony Richmond's rich, eccentric uncle Charles is found murdered, suspicion immediately focuses on the old man's widow, Maria, who had been his nurse. Anthony, in fact, had persuaded her to marry Charles, with a plan to lay his hands on the old man's money. The problem was that Maria had grown genuinely fond of her husband, and following his death, she realizes that Anthony is responsible and has been using her to achieve his own purposes. Maria is accused of the crime and Anthony does nothing to help her. Only at the very last minute do the police find evidence of Maria's innocence and Anthony's guilt.

BACKGROUND AND REVIEWS

A routine melodrama that has the attraction of including in the cast Sean Connery, in between James Bond roles. Audiences were curious to see the actor in a different role and enthusiastically greeted both *Woman of Straw* and Lumet's *The Hill* (1965). But unfortunately Dearden's film goes no further. It is irredeemably mediocre, as indeed is Gina Lollobrigida's acting.

"A trio of handsome and skillful performers, and some perfectly lovely sets and scenery in the English countryside and on the island of Majorca are the principal features of [the film]. But once you get past these, I'm afraid there's very little else to hold your attention...[but] it's nice to see Miss Lollobrigida lounging about in low-cut lingerie." (Leo Mishkin, *New York Morning Telegraph,* 1 October 1964).

"Gina Lollobrigida, Sean Connery and Sir Ralph Richardson add up to a trio of marquee names sufficiently intriguing to [offer] valuable lures for the crowds. But it is unlikely that customers will work up much enthusiasm for this plodding meller-murder [film] which rolls to a preposterous climax....Miss Lollobrigida, when not changing her high-class duds, is out of her depth in what must be a serious role if it is to jell." (*Variety,* 6 May 1964).

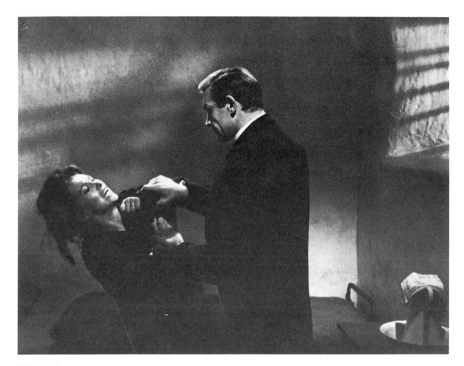

With Sean Connery.

With Sean Connery and Ralph Richardson.

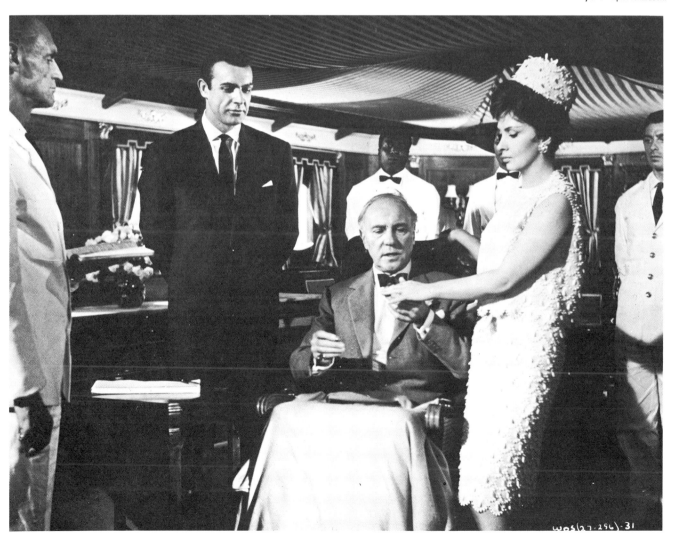

With Rock Hudson and Gig Young.

Strange Bedfellows (Strani compagni di letto)

1964

Produced by Norman Panama and Melvin Frank for Panama/Frank Productions. Director: Melvin Frank. Story: Norman Panama and Melvin Frank. Screenplay: Melvin Frank and Michael Pertwee. Photography: Leo Tover (Technicolor). Music: Leigh Harline. Art director: Alexander Golitzen. Editor: Gene Milford. Gina Lollobrigida's gowns: Jean Louis. Distribution: Universal. Origin: USA. Running time 98 minutes.

CAST

Rock Hudson (Carter Harrison), Gina Lollobrigida (Toni Vincente), Gig Young (Richard Bramwell), Edward Judd (Harry Jones), Terry Thomas (Assistant mortician), Arthur Haynes (Chauffeur), Howard St. John (J. L. Stevens), David King (Taxi driver), Peggy Rea (Mavis), Joseph Sirola (Petracini), Nancy Kulp (Aggressive woman), Lucy Landau (Jolly woman), Bernard Fox (Policeman), Edith Atwater (Mrs. Stevens), James MacCallion (Old man), Hadley Mattingly (Bagshott), John Orchard (Radio dispatcher), Frederic Worlock (Lawyer), Alan Caillou (Magistrate), Arthur Gould Porter (Chief mortician).

SYNOPSIS

American executive Carter and his fiery Italian wife Toni have been unable to live together for years, due to Toni's devil-may-care character. When he finds himself up for an important promotion, his chances depend on his being reconciled with his wife. Not without difficulty, Carter manages to rekindle the old flame but then Toni, who has not changed one bit, still up to cham-

With Rock Hudson.

pioning minority causes, takes part in a parade, riding naked through the streets of Soho like Lady Godiva! For poor Carter it is almost the end of his career, but he perseveres in wooing Toni back, and she repents, patches up her quarrel with her husband and promises to behave herself in the future.

BACKGROUND AND REVIEWS

This light-hearted film was made in the wake of the success achieved by Mulligan's *Come September*. The same co-stars, same producers. "La Lollo", as in the earlier film, and in *Buona Sera, Mrs. Campbell,* is perfectly at ease in this type of comedy, in which she plays the part of a fiery, quarrelsome, obstinate, unpredictable woman.

"The fact that [the leads] are played by Rock Hudson and Gina Lollobrigida is assurance enough that [the characters] are as obvious and unsurprising as peas in a plushy pod. [Co-screenwriter] Melvin Frank, who also directed, is an ordinarily witty man. But he and his collaborator have been sparing wit and humor here. Miss Lollobrigida is handsome in a variety of slacks and negligees, but she is not a magician. She can't do much without a script." (Bosley Crowther, *The New York Times,* 11 March 1965).

"Rock and Gina need no introduction. Neither is the world's greatest farceur, but each is learning, ambitious, and not without personal qualifications for the job. Rock is always just stuffy enough to be an exec, just charming enough to please an audience. Lollo always has that look—the one that makes you keep on looking." (Archer Winsten, *New York Post,* 11 March 1965)

"Miss Lollobrigida has, need we note, photogenic decolletage, and some of the players have ability that is, apparently, unphotographable." (*New York Herald-Tribune,* 11 March 1965).

"The variations, some more outre than others, on the theme of the marriage bed, have become a standard in Hollywood ever since this 'nouvelle vague' reached the American shores. Leaving aside the actors for a moment, there is nothing to justify the making of such a banal, unimaginative movie." (Anonymous, *Cinéma,* n. 98, July-August 1965).

"Once again, the theme is divorce, but here this deconsecrated reality of modern society is very artificially embalmed and the lack of imagination corresponds to a lack of necessity. Moreover, Gina does not sparkle enough in her role. But we have seen worse of its kind." (Michel Delahaye, *Cahiers du Cinéma,* year XV, n. 168, July 1965).

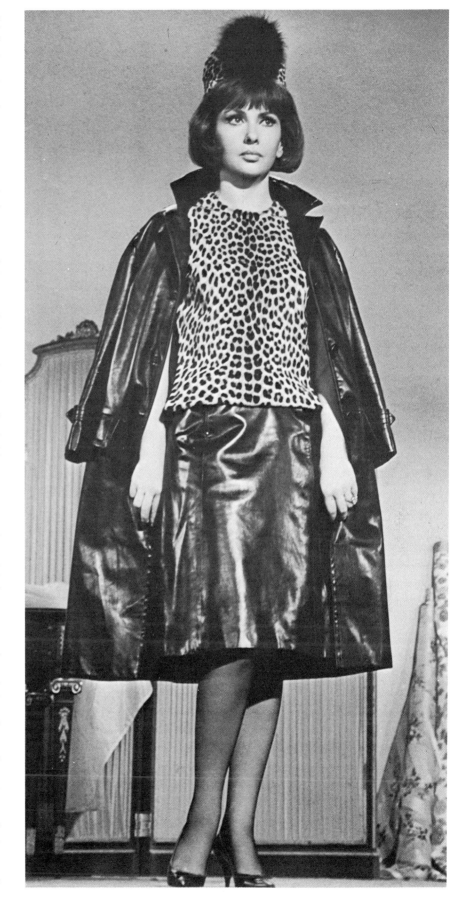

Le bambole (The Dolls)

1964

Episode: *Monsignor Cupido*
Produced by Gianni Hecht Lucari for Documento Films. Director: Mauro Bolognini. From a story in the *Decameron*. Screenplay: Leo Benvenuti and Pietro De Bernardi. Photography: Leonida Barboni. (b/w). Music: Armando Trovajoli. Art director: Gianni Polidori. Editor: Roberto Cinguini. Costumes: Piero Tosi. Distribution: Columbia-Ceiad. Origin: Italy. French title: *Les poupées*. English title: *Four Kinds of Love*.

CAST

Gina Lollobrigida (Beatrice), Jean Sorel (Vincenzo), Akim Tamiroff (Monsignor Arcudi), Gianni Rizzo (hotel manager), Camillo Milli.
The other three episodes were: Dino Risi's *La telefonata,* Luigi Comencini's *Il trattato di Eugenetica* and Franco Rossi's *La minestra*.

SYNOPSIS

Beatrice, a hotel-owner's sex-starved wife falls in love with the nephew of a monsignore. In order to arouse the interests of the young man, she adroitly takes advantage of the priest's gullibility.

BACKGROUND AND REVIEWS

Le bambole is one of "La Lollo's" rare appearances in a new-style Italian comedy. It is a pity that Risi, Scola, Monicelli, Age and Scarpelli did not have more opportunity to work with her. There was, at one point, a Monicelli project, also to be called *Le bambole,* which was to star Lollobrigida and Silvana Mangano, but it was abandoned. Such a pity, as it would have given Gina the opportunity, after her successful Hollywood interlude, to work with some of the big stars of Italian comedy. The episode in this sex comedy entitled *Monsignor Cupido* shows just how self-possessed Gina had become in this type of role.

"The film apparently caused a small scandal in Italy, though its aim was really nothing more than to infringe, ironically or maliciously depending on the episode, certain transalpine taboos (small ones at that). But *I mostri* and *Alta fedeltà* did the same thing in a more amusing, more impertinent way .... Bolognini's episode is favoured by the powerful acting of Akim Tamiroff, anxious, noble and moving beneath his ecclesiastical robes which he seems to have worn all his life. A slimmer, befeathered Gina Lollobrigida is good as the female lead, Jean Sorel is not bad." (Jean-André, *Cahiers du cinéma*, year XV, n. 169, August 1965).

"Gina Lollobrigida is fine as the beauty with designs, Jean Sorel makes an okay target of her attention." (Hawk, *Variety*, 3 February 1965)

I remember that *Le bambole* had a spot of bother with the censor and it was even accused of offending decency! But it was not withdrawn from the market.

With Jean Sorel and Akim Tamiroff.

Io, io, io…e gli altri (Me, Me, Me…and the Others)

1966

Produced by Luigi Rovere for Cineluxor/Rizzoli Film (Rome). Director: Alessandro Blasetti. Story: Alessandro Blasetti and Carlo Romano. Screenplay: Alessandro Blasetti, Carlo Romano in collaboration with Agenore Incrocci, Furio Scarpelli, Adriano Baracco, Leo Benvenuti, Piero De Bernardi, Lianella Carell, Suso Cecchi D'Amico, Ennio Flaiano, Giorgio Rossi, Libero Solaroli, Vincenzo Talarico. Photography: Aldo Giordani. (b/w). Music: Carlo Rustichelli. Art directors: Dario Cecchi and Ottavio Scotti. Editor: Tatiana Casini. Costumes: Milena Bonomo. Distribution: Cineriz. Origin: Italy. Running time 120 minutes.

CAST

Walter Chiari (Sandro), Gina Lollobrigida (Titta, his wife), Vittorio De Sica (Commendator Trepossi), Silvana Mangano (Silvia), Marcello Mastroianni (Peppino Marassi) Nino Manfredi (Sleeping car attendant), Elisa Cegani (Peppino's housekeeper), Caterina Boratto (Luigia, Peppino's sister-in-law), Grazia Maria Spina (Peppino's niece), Vittorio Caprioli (Politician), Mario Pisu (Winner of the "Capranica"), Paolo Panelli (Photographer), Lelio Luttazzi (Director), Elio Pandolfi (Newscaster), Mario Valdemarin (Waiter in the restaurant car), Fanfulla (Concierge), Giustino Durano (Policeman), Sylva Koscina (the "Star"), Mario Scaccia (Journalist), Andrea Checchi (Praying man), Saro Urzi (Second praying man), Umberto D'Orsi (Man in the train), Carlo Croccolo (Another traveller), Graziella Granata (Girl on the train), Salvo Randone (Traveller with a menu), Marisa Merlini (Lady on the telephone), Luisa Rivelli (Lady dancing), Gianni Rizzo, Nerio Bernardi, Mimmo Poli, Marina Malfatti, Daniela Surina, Pietro Pastore, Silvio Bagolini, Francesco Baiolo, Renato Caizzi Terra, Salvatore Campochiaro, Enzo Cerusico, Alberto Cevenini, Solveig D'Assunta, Ermelinda De Felice, Rica Dialina, Rossana Di Rocco, Maria Rosaria Di Pietro, Alessandro Dori, Mario Ferrari, Ettore Geri, Charles John Karlsen, Renato Malavasi, Gianni Manera, Geneviève Mark, Vittorio Mazza, Fabrizio Mononi, Paul Muller, Lia Murano, Enzo Petito, Umberto Sacripante, Rosella Spinelli, Carlo Sposito, Tellino Tellini, Giulio Tomassini, Elsa Vazzoler, Luigi Visconti, Leena von Martens, Antoinette Weynen.

SYNOPSIS

Sandro, a journalist, is gathering anecdotes, true stories and information in general on the egotism of the human race and man's indifference to others. To do this he first analyses himself and the people nearest and dearest to him. The film is thus composed of innumerable episodes, some very brief, revealing this particular aspect of the human nature, along with a host of star cameos. Above all, the story underlines Sandro's relationship with his wife Titti, his mistress Silvia and his friend Peppino.

The same reception which *Le Bambole* received greeted this film. Under the direction of Blasetti, Gina Lollobrigida gave the best performance of her later career. The scene with Walter Chiari in the bedroom, with some accomplished acting on both sides, is amusing and complies intelligently with Blasetti's intentions.

BACKGROUND AND REVIEWS

"*Io, io, io…e gli altri* marked Blasetti's official retirement from the screen. The object of the film was to attack egotism…none of us are free from this flaw, and no circumstance exists that does not provoke it, said Blasetti. A large section of the Italian cinema world, including screenwriters, technicians and actors too, decided to wish him farewell by lending their services for nothing…As regards Walter Chiari, this is perhaps his toughest and most gratifying screen role…

With Walter Chiari.

Lollobrigida played the perfidious wife, maliciously aware of her influence over her husband, and with an idea all of her own as to the meaning of jealousy and pride." (Vice, *Corriere della Sera,* 17 February 1966).

"The sharp little darts (of Blasetti's film) have a definite target: egotism appears in an endless variety of forms in contemporary society, from it arise innumerable evils, by-products they might be called, such as arrogance, hypocricy, narcissism, fanaticism...Consequently, it has been necessary to split the film, the object of which is to ridicule all this, into many episodes...Not an easy task, to be sure, and not all the material thus put together is equally successful." (Guglielmo Biraghi, *Il Messaggero,* 26 February 1966).

"The real trouble with this contemporary morality tale is that it never finds a level consistent with its theme. Broad comedy in the loquacious Italian manner is awkwardly juxtaposed with what are little more than platitudes masquerading as profundities." (*Monthly Film Bulletin,* March 1968).

L'amante italiana (The Sultans)

With Louis Jourdan.

1966

Produced by Alvaro Mancori – Jacques-Paul Bertrand – Cineurop. Director: Jean Delannoy. From the novel *Les sultans* by Christiane De Rivoyre. Screenplay: De Rivoyre, Delannoy, and Jean-Loup Debadie. Photography: Tonino Delli Colli (Eastmancolor). Music: Georges Gavarentz. Editor: Henri Taverna. Distribution: Indipendenti regionali. Origin: France/Italy. French title: *Les sultans.*

CAST

Gina Lollobrigida (Lisa), Louis Jourdan (Laurent), Philippe Noiret (Michou), Corinne Marchand (Mireille), Muriel Baptiste (Kim), Daniel Gelin (Leo), Renée Faure (Odette), Claude Gensac (Model), Rosy Varte (Girl in the club), Lucia Modugno.

SYNOPSIS

Lisa, a fashion photographer living in Paris, returns home after work one day to find that her married lover, Laurent, is not waiting for her as usual.

119

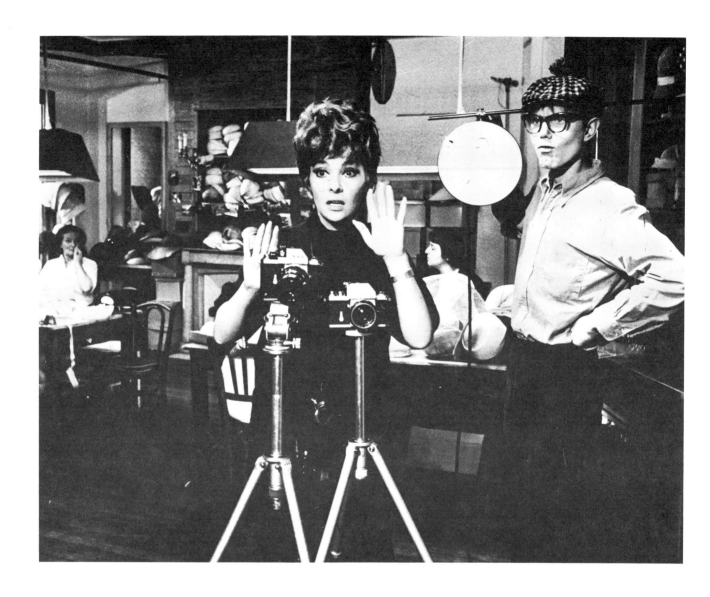

Passing the time chatting with a giddy neighbor, Mireille, Lisa gets word from a girlfriend who had spotted Laurent in a night club in the company of a young girl. Lisa tries to commit suicide, but Mireille and her friend Michou manage to prevent her from doing so. Next day, Laurent explains to Lisa that the girl in the night club was, in reality, his daughter Kim, who has become involved with an older man. Laurent is worried about Kim and that evening he again leaves Lisa and goes off to keep a watchful eye on his daughter. Once alone, Lisa calls Mireille and together they discuss men, reaching the conclusion that perhaps they too have a right to have problems of their own.

BACKGROUND AND REVIEWS

"Why use the plural in the title? Why *The Sultans?*" One sultan (insulting) would have been quite sufficient! Insulting because it is stupid and vulgar, while Gina Lollobrigida beats all records for utter nonsense, the record previously being held by Melina Mercouri for her role in Bardem's *Les pianos mécaniques*. From a polished little novel by Christiane de Rivoyre, on the question of adultery, Delannoy has made this ridiculous film, which has none of the book's bitter charm, but instead has all its conventions." (Pierre Billard, *Cinéma 66*, n. 107, June 1966).

"A prodigiously hypocritical view of the relationship between man and woman. The 'cocotte' who passively awaits some favor to be dispensed by her lover exists only in Christiane de Rivoyre's and Jean-Loup Debadie's screenplay. And as for young girls who require a father's helping hand, they are even rarer! There is perhaps one interesting point in this irritating serial story: a flashback in which Delannoy par-odies Chris Marker's *La Jetée* and other short films inspired by the 'fotoromanzi'." (Michel Mardore, *Cahiers du Cinema,* year XVI, n. 179, 1966).

"Seems like an updated version of that perennial tearjerker *Back Street,* with an added dollop of French frankness, but its insights into behavior are slight and the characters fairly trivial, without depth as to social backgrounds." (Mosk., *Variety,* 1 June 1966)

Hotel Paradiso

1966

Produced by Peter Glenville for MGM.
Director: Peter Glenville. Story and
screenplay: Peter Glenville and Jean-
Claude Carrière from the comedy
L'hotel du libre echange by Georges
Feydeau. Photography: Henri Decae
(Metrocolor-Panavision). Music: Lau-
rence Rosenthal. Art director: Jacques
Dupont. Editor: Anne V. Coates. Dis-
tribution: Metro-Goldwyn-Mayer. Origin:
Great Britain. Running time: 99
minutes.

CAST

Alec Guinness (Benedict Boniface),
Gina Lollobrigida (Marcelle Cot),

With Alec Guinness.

ALEC GUINNESS et GINA LOLLOBRIGIDA
dans UN FILM DE PETER GLENVILLE
PARADISO, HOTEL DU LIBRE ECHANGE
d'après la pièce · L'Hôtel du Libre Echange · de Georges Feydeau et Maurice Desvallières
avec ROBERT MORLEY
DARIO MORENO
avec la participation de MARIE BELL et AKIM TAMIROFF
Scénario de PETER GLENVILLE et JEAN-CLAUDE CARRIERE · Production et réalisation de PETER GLENVILLE
Directeur de la Photographie HENRI DECAE · Producteur associé PIERRE JOURDAN

With Alec Guinness.

Feydeau's timely appearance on the scene saves the maid from becoming the general scapegoat.

BACKGROUND AND REVIEWS

In 1956, director-producer Peter Glenville brilliantly brought to the stage Georges Feydeau's comedy *Hotel du libre echange*. He apparently thought he need do no more than thin out the original script here and there, add one or two innovations, such as the police chase, so dear to the silent screen, and the appearance of Feydeau in search of ideas, in order to create a very amusing film. And as Glenville is above all a theatre man, he decided to retain the exuberant, parodic tone of the original, so typical of vaudville." (Anonymous, *L'Unità*, 20 October 1966).

"An old-fashioned rumpus stirred-up by a would-be philanderer and the pretty wife of his next-door neighbor was meant to be a silent movie. Expanded to the screen in an elegant color package, it remains a play only slightly disguised for the screen by the lacquered direction of Peter Glenville…Miss Lollobrigida is, of course, most desirable as the Pouting Potential Adulteress." (Kathleen Carroll, New York *Daily News*, 15 October 1966).

Miss Lollobrigida, who is inclined to be flamboyant and expansive, does not mesh too easily with the style maintained by the others." (Thomas Lask, *The New York Times*, 15 October 1966).

"Gina Lollobrigida is impossibly beautiful, and no one expects her to be funny. She isn't. But when actors like Alec Guinness, Robert Morley and Akim Tamiroff aren't funny either, something is drastically wrong….Nowhere is there the inspired madness that Bert Lahr and Angela Lansbury brought to the Broadway version." (William Pepper, New York *World-Journal-Tribune*, 15 October 1966).

Robert Morley (Henri Cot), Peggy Mount (Angelique Boniface), Marie Bell (Silent screen star), Akim Tamiroff (Aniello), Derek Fowles (Maxime), Ann Beach (Victoire) Leonard Rossiter (Inspector), Douglas Byng (Mr. Martin), Peter Glenville (Georges Feydeau), Robertson Hare (Duke), Edra Gale, Dario Moreno.

SYNOPSIS

The story of the film is that of Feydeau's comedy, but with the additional character of the writer himself who, by secretly observing the behavior of his neighbors (it is Paris in 1910), bit by bit puts together his play. We have Marcelle who is misbehaving with Benedict just to annoy her husband Henri, while Henri's nephew is carrying on with Marcelle's maid. We have a number of "convenient" departures: Henri on business, Benedict's wife to visit a sick friend, or so they say. Of course, all our characters turn up at the Hotel Paradise, to the embarrassment of everyone. A police raid finally puts an end to all the goings on, and

Le avventure e gli amori di Miguel Cervantes (The Adventures and Loves of Miguel Cervantes)

1966

Produced by Alexander Salkind for Protor Film (Rome) – Prisma Film (Madrid) – Procinex (Paris). Director: Vincent Sherman. From the novel by Bruno Franck. Screenplay: Enrique Llovet and Henry Bay. Photography: Edmund Richard (Supertotalvision 70mm—Eastmancolor). Music: Jean Ledrut. Art directors: Enrique Allaçcon and Luciano De Nardi. Costumes: Luis Arguello. Editor: Marguerite Ochoa. Distribution: Independenti regionali. Origin: Italy/France/Spain. Running time: 119 minutes. American title: *The Young Rebel*. English title: *Cervantes*.

CAST

Horst Buchholz (Miguel de Cervantes), Gina Lollobrigida (Giulia Toffolo), Louis Jourdan (Cardinal Acquaviva), José Ferrer (Hassam Bey), Francisco Rabal (Rodrigo Cervantes), Fernando Rey (Philip II), Soledad Miranda (Nessa), Antonio Casas, Angel Del Pozo, Ricardo Balacios, Maurice de Canonge, José Jaspe, Claudine Dalmas, José Nieto, Enzo Curcio, Gaudenzio Di Pietro, Andres Mejuto.
Note: In the American version, David Karp is credited with the screenplay.

SYNOPSIS

The film relates numerous episodes from the adventurous life of the creator of *Don Quixote*. As a young man, Cervantes becomes secretary to Monsignor Acquaviva, Papal envoy to the court of Philip II, and goes to live in Rome. On his way, he meets and falls in love with Giulia Toffolo, unaware that she is one of Rome's leading courtesans and is soon to be banished from the city by the Pope. Cervantes is appointed as guide to the Turkish sultan's envoy in Rome. Hassam Bey rescues him from a brawl with the help of Giulia's servants, but with Giulia's expulsion Cervantes decides to join the army. He takes part in the battle of Lepanto during which he is wounded, and is taken to Messina where, for the last time, he meets Giulia, who is living at court. But he is soon called back into action, is taken prisoner by Arab pirates, and finally released when Hassam is appointed governor of Algiers. It is during this troubled period that he meets a Span-

With Horst Buchholz.

ish girl named Nessa, on whom he later based the *Don Quixote* character of Dulcinea.

BACKGROUND AND REVIEWS

"Prepared initially by King Vidor, the film was eventually taken over by Vincent Sherman, assisted by one or two hangers-on. The director merits nothing but reproach, while the screenplay gives a hint of what the film might have been in Vidor's hands: for instance, the beauty of some of the scenes (the meeting between Philip II and Cer-

vantes, the fine performance given by some of the actors (Gina Lollobrigida plays a role similar to the one she had in *Solomon and Sheba)* and lastly the realism of certain human conflicts (the relationship between Cervantes and José Ferrer's Hassam Bey). Unfortunately, the emptiness of Horst Buchholz's acting, worse than usual, is a grave handicap." (Patrick Brion, *Cahiers du Cinéma*, year XVIII, n. 200/201, April-May 1968).

"From his native Spain to Algeria, from the palace to the battle of Lepanto, the life of Don Quixote's future creator has all that it needs to arouse

the imagination. Basically, it means counter-balancing, or rather uniting, the man of action and the man of intellect, the artist and the soldier, the poet and the military man. King Vidor, who was to have directed the film, spent many months on its preparation. Little remains of his work, though on occasions the screenplay gives some hint... As it is, Sherman's film is a succession of images without life, ugly images, badly edited. The catastrophe has one or two redeeming features: the battle of Lepanto, Gina Lollobrigida's departure, Cervantes' imprisonment." (Bernard Cohn, *Positif,* n. 95, May 1968).

I fear that there is little else to add. Vincent Sherman was another of those aging directors who had occasion to work with Lollobrigida at the close of their careers. It happened with Siodmak, Robert Z. Leonard (who made only two more films after *La donna più bella del mondo*) and with King Vidor, who retired from the screen with *Solomon and Sheba*. (Another old master of motion pictures, George Cukor, also had a brush with Gina. It was for *Lady L* which, in view of the strained relations between actress and director, was abandoned. It was made at a later date by Peter Ustinov and starred Sophia Loren.) Sherman too — former actor of the 1930s, who directed Rita Hayworth in *Affair in Trinidad* — said his farewells to the screen with *Cervantes*.

Le piacevoli notti (Pleasant Nights)

1966

Produced by Mario Cecchi Gori for Fair Film. Directors: Armando Crispino and Luciano Lucignani. Story: Steno. Screenplay: Alessandro Continenza. Photography: Enrico Menczer, Leonida Barboni, Gabor Pogany (Eastmancolor). Music: Gino Marinuzzi, Jr. Art direction and costumes: Pierluigi Pizzi. Editor: Marcello Malvestiti. Distribution: Titanus. Origin: Italy.

CAST OF THE SECOND STORY:

Gina Lollobrigida (Domicilla), Adolfo Celi (Bernadozzo), Daniele Vargas (Fortebraccio da Montone), Eros Pagni (Soldier).

Vittorio Gassman, Ugo Tognazzi, Maria Grazia Buccella, Magda Konopka, Gigi Ballista, Filippo Scelzo, Ida Galli, Luigi Vannucchi, Dante Posani, Luigi Proietti, Ernesto Colli, Glauco Onorato.

SYNOPSIS

The film consists of three stories linked one to another by the journey undertaken by Pope Giulio II and his retinue. In reality, it is only the painter Bastiano di Sangallo disguised as the Pope. Lollobrigida appears in the second tale, playing Domicilla, wife of Bernadozzo the astrologer, who begs the Pope's pardon for having had unchaste dreams. The false Pope absolves her and tells her to carry on dreaming and not to worry about it.

REVIEWS

" 'Prosaic and materialistic' is how the Italian writer, philosopher and literary critic Francesco De Sanctis described the 16th .century novelist Straparola, author of a collection of stories entitled *Le piacevoli notti*. The title and one or two hints are all that remain of the book in this jocular, vulgar, goliardic film. The episode starring the resplendent Gina Lollobrigida is the best, also from a figurative point of view, and is more reminiscent of the paintings of that era than the others." (Aldo Scagnetti, *Paese Sera*, 24 September 1966).

"Pleasant too are the mornings, afternoons and evenings of this 15th century Tuscany, with their fleeting love affairs and vicious pranks. The bright Technicolor photography makes each scene seem like a 15th century miniature, depicting the painter Bastiano di Sangallo, a fake Julius II and an equally fake Lucrezia Borgia…but above all a multitude of beautiful women, including Gina Lollobrigida and Maria Grazia Buccella, starring beside Vittorio Gassman and Ugo Tognazzi. Crispino and Lucignani have directed this lascivious affair with a subtle and delicate touch." (Vice, *Il Messaggero*, 24 September 1966).

With Adolfo Celi.

La morte ha fatto l'uovo (Death Lays An Egg)

1967

Produced by Franco Marras for Summa Cinematografic/Cine Azimut (Rome)—Les Films Corona (France). Director: Giulio Questi. Story and screenplay: Giulio Questi and Franco Arcalli. Photography: Dario De Palma (Technicolor – Techniscope). Music: Bruno Maderna. Art director: Sergio Canevari. Editor: Franco Arcalli. Distribution: Euro International Films. Origin: Italy/France. Running time: 105 minutes. French title: *La mort a pondu un oeuf*. English title: *A Curious Way to Love*. American title: *Plucked*.

CAST

Gina Lollobrigida (Anna), Jean-Louis Trintignant (Marco), Ewa Aulin (Gabri), Jean Sobieski (Mondaini), Renato Romano (Luigi), Giulio Donnini (Hotel manager), Vittorio André, Biagio Pelligra, Ugo Adinolfi, Cleofe Del Cile, Conrad Andersen, Lisa Ferrero, Monica Millesi.

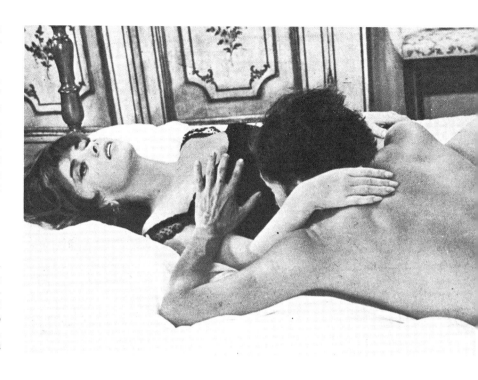

With Jean-Louis Trintignant.

SYNOPSIS

Marco, a chicken breeder dominated by his beautiful wife, falls in love with his wife's niece, Gabri, who has come to stay with them. But Gabri too has another relationship, with a cynical man named Mondaini, and together they conspire to eliminate Marco and Anna and inherit the farm. By means of an anonymous letter, they lure Anna to a motel and there murder her, planning to pin the crime on Marco, but he discovers the body and decides to dispose of it by throwing it into a mill. In doing so, he accidentally slips, falls into his chicken-food machinery and is killed. Gabri and her lover gloat over their easy victory, without realizing that Anna's body is still where Marco left it. The body is discovered and the two are arrested for the crime—and for murdering Marco as well.

126

BACKGROUND AND REVIEWS

This is another of those films that seem to have been made to intentionally irritate the Italian critics, the official ones that is, who had yet to be jolted by the forced "discovery" of American cinema—none too easily digested, even today. *La morte ha fatto l'uovo* is an exercise in the thriller, cynically and amusingly conducted and which, had it succeeded, would have provided some interesting food for thought. Questi's film was probably made too early, if not for the public, then for the press, who were noticeably ill at ease, though impressed by the professionalism of the director (author of *Se sei vivo spara* 1967, *Arcana* 1972) ably assisted by co-screenwriter and editor, Franco Arcalli.

"There can be no doubt that Questi's work is refined and intelligent, that he knows by heart the subtle tricks of his trade as, with complete self-confidence, he mingles his own personal characterizations with references to other directors: Antonioni, Godard and even Jessua are continually echoed and engulfed in a ka-leidoscopic journey which leaves no stone unturned in its effort to 'delight.' Lollobrigida and Trintignan, having little incentive to go beyond the realms of the 'star system,' are opaque and they even fail to stay the distance..." (Claudio Bertieri, *Cinema 60,* year IX, n. 69, 1968.).

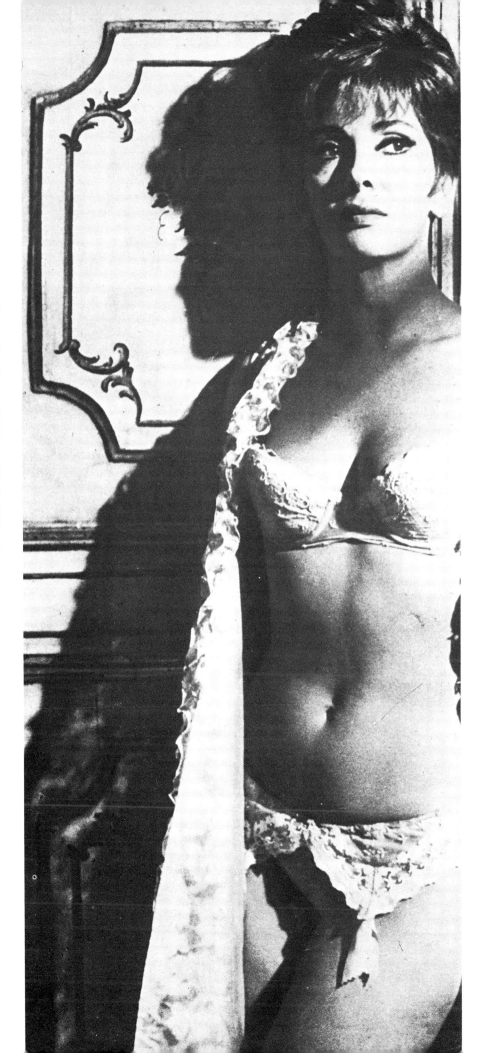

The Private Navy of Sergeant O'Farrell (Mash – La guerra privata del sergente O'Farrell)

1967

With Bob Hope.

Produced by John Beck – Naho Production for United Artists. Director: Frank Tashlin. Story: John L. Greene and Robert M. Fresco. Screenplay: Frank Tashlin. Photography: Alan Stensvold (Technicolor). Music: Harry Sukman. Editor: Ronald Sinclair. Distribution: Indipendenti regionali. Origin: USA. Running time: 92 minutes. American title: *The Private Navy of Sgt. O'Farrell*. French title: *Le Marine en folie*.

CAST

Bob Hope (Master Sergeant Dan O'Farrell), Phyllis Diller (Nurse Nellie Krause), Jeffrey Hunter (Lt. [J.G.] Lyman P. Jones), Gina Lollobrigida (Maria), Mylène Demongeot (Gaby), John Myhere (Lt. Comm. Roger Snavely), Mako (Calvin Coolidge Ishimura), Henry Wilcoxon (Rear Adm. Arthur L. Stokes), Dick Sargent (Capt. Elwood Prohaska), Christopher Dark (Strongbow), Michael Burns (Bannon), William Wellmann, Jr. (Kennedy), Robert Donner (Ogg), Jack Grinnage (Roberts), William Christopher (Schultz), John Spina (Miller).
Note: The credits said: "and Miss Gina Lollobrigida as Maria."

SYNOPSIS

A group of American soldiers, confined to a rather monotonous existence on a small Pacific island, are afflicted by an acute lack of alcohol and women! Their sergeant, Dan O'Farrell, decides that it is high time somebody did something about it. He asks for some nurses to be sent out, but only one arrives, nurse Nellie Krause, and she is hardly the world's most beautiful creature. O'Farrell has more luck with the alcohol, when he finds a crate of beer on the beach, washed up from a ship that has been sunk in action. Later on, he has even better luck when he saves two shipwrecked beauties on a raft. Maria and Gaby are both young and ravishing, and their presence on the island at last livens up the soldiers' daily routine, and decidedly lifts morale.

BACKGROUND AND REVIEWS

The name of Frank Tashlin, director of this comedy-vehicle for Bob Hope, is remembered in particular for his long-lasting association with Jerry Lewis: *Artists and Models* (1955), *The Geisha Boy* (1958), *Cinderfella* (1960) and *Who's Minding the Store* (1963), and so forth. Films of a certain prestige for all comedy lovers and fans of Jerry Lewis, whose destructive abilities were always especially successful under Tashlin's direction. But this is a film starring Bob Hope—who previously had worked with Tashlin in *Son of Paleface* (1952)—and it is quite a different matter. Here, the comedy is mainly verbal with frequent reference to earlier motion picture situations. What about Gina? She was making a guest appearance and her portrayal differed little from those given under the direction of Melvin Frank (who also wrote scripts for and directed Bob Hope): ability, self-assurance, charm.

The film was not released in Italy until eight years later and at the end of the season. "A typical summer film...from a director who, in happier moments, has given us comedies worthy of a certain merit (his best are those starring Jerry Lewis)...The insipid story is enriched, if enriched is the right word, by a series of repartees frequently dubbed with considerable bad taste. (Aurora Santuari, *Paese Sera*, 28 May 1975).

"Gina Lollobrigida provides the glamor. Director Frank Tashlin keeps the gags going and wins special mention for a sequence between Bob Hope and Miss Lollobrigida. They do a take-off on the love scene between Burt Lancaster and Deborah Kerr in *From Here to Eternity* [and] as a huge wave engulfs the couple on the beach, Hope comes up choking. The comedy has enough nonsense to be generally amusing." (Ann Guarino, New York *Daily News*, 9 May 1968)

"A Bob Hope vehicle that carries him to a Pacific island for World War II shenanigans with Phyllis Diller, the Navy, the Army and a lone friendly American-born Japanese in enemy uniform. Some of the pressure for departure is lifted when Gina Lollobrigida and Mylene Demongeot show up in believe-it-or-not style." (Archer Winsten, *New York Post*, 9 May 1968)

Buona Sera, Mrs. Campbell (Buonasera, signora Campbell)

1968

Produced by Melvin Frank for Connaught Productions/United Artists. Director: Melvin Frank. Story and screenplay: Melvin Frank, Denis Norden, Sheldon Keller. Photography: Gabor Pogany (Technicolor). Music: Riz Ortolani. Art director: Arrigo Equini. Editor: William Butler. Distribution: United Artists. Origin: USA. Running time: 113 minutes. American title: *Buona sera, Mrs. Campbell*. French title: *Bonsoir Mrs. Campbell*.

CAST

Gina Lollobrigida (Carla Campbell), Shelley Winters (Shirley Newman), Phil Silvers (Phil Newman), Peter Lawford (Justin Young), Telly Savalas (Walter Braddock), Lee Grant (Frizie Braddock), Janet Margolin (Gia), Marian Moses (Lauren Young), Philippe Leroy (Vittorio), Naomi Stevens (Rosa), Giovanna Galletti (Countess), Renzo Palmer (Mayor), Dale Cummings (Pete),

James Mishler (Stubby).
Awards: Gina Lollobrigida won a "David di Donatello."

SYNOPSIS

In the small town of San Forino, during the American occupation of Italy, Carla was "sentimentally involved" with three G.I.'s, Phil, Justin and Walter. Some months later, the war over, and

With Telly Savalas, Peter Lawford and Phil Silvers.

the three men having departed for their homeland, Carla gives birth to a little girl, Gia. She does not know who the father is, but writes to all three and from all three, over the years, receives money to bring the child up. When Gia becomes a teenager, Carla tells her that her father died heroically in the war. One day, the old regiment, back in Italy on a tour, turns up in San Forino, and with it Gia's three fathers and their American wives. Each of the men is convinced that he is the father and each, when he meets Carla again, tries to pick up the relationship where he left off. The situation becomes more and more complicated and in the end all three have to admit defeat.

With Telly Savalas.

With Philippe Leroy.

This is the most popular of Gina Lollobrigida's Hollywood movies. In fact, in America she is often remembered for her role as Mrs. Campbell. The character is reminiscent of Anna of Brooklyn and there is a certain similarity between the two Italian villages that provide the background. The most important factor in the enormous popularity of this film is that Gina, who is just as the Americans imagine an Italian woman to be, is acting with Americans with whom the audience can readily identify themselves. In other words, Gina is the equivalent of those architectonic beauties of Negulesco's *Three Coins in a Fountain* and other films about tourists in Italy.

"Don't take your stopwatch to clock your laughs because they come one a minute in this lively frolic on the advantages of being an unwed mother with one, two, three men, each thinking he is the father of a beautiful daughter. . . . beautiful Gina is good at comedy timing." (Wanda Hale, New York *Daily News,* 13 February 1969).

"This overcooked, hardbreathing frolic, which gets off to a bright start, eventually collapses in the category of impossible comedies, sniggeringly pegged to sex . . . the reasonable taste, the bounce and the logic all start floundering about mid-point, with everyone running wildly to catch up, including poor Miss Lollobrigida, who bears the brunt of the confusion and the redundant contrivances. Suddenly it is gags, gags and more gags, to no avail, until the plot peg of authentic paternity begins to sound like a tired old burlesque joke." (Howard Thompson, *The New York Times*, 13 February 1969).

Un bellissimo novembre (A Beautiful November)

1968

Produced by Adelphia Compagnia Cinematografica (Rome) / Les Productions Artistes Associes (Paris). Director: Mauro Bolognini. From the novel by Ercole Patti. Screenplay: Lucia Drudi Demby, Antonio Altoviti, Henry Vaughn. Photography: Armando Nannuzzi (Technicolor). Music: Ennie Morricone. Art director: Vanni Castellani. Costumes: Cesare Rovatti. Editor: Roberto Perpignani. Distribution: Dear Film / UA. Origin: Italy/France. French title: *Ce merveilleux automne*. American title: *That Splendid November*.

With Paolo Turco.

With Andre Laurence.

CAST

Gina Lollobrigida (Cettina), Gabriele Ferzetti (Biagio), André Laurence (Sasà), Paolo Turco (Nino), Margarita Lozano (Amalia), Danielle Godet (Elisa), Isabella Savona (Giulietta), Corrado Gaipa (Uncle Alfio), Jean Mancorps (Mimi), Pasquale Fortunato (Umberto), Ileana Riganò (Rosaria), Grazia Di Marzo (Assurta), Franco Abbinia (Enzo), Maria Di Benedetto (Aunt Tecia), Ettore Ribotta (Corcetto), Vanni Castellani (Turiddu), Amalia Troiani (Aunt Maria), Maria Rosa Amato (Juzza), Giuseppe Naso (Uncle Nicola).
Note: Gina Lollobrigida is dubbed by Rita Savagnone.

SYNOPSIS

Nino, a lonely teenager, feels that no one has ever understood him. The only person with whom he experiences a certain affinity is his beautiful aunt Cettina, over whom he begins to lust. Cettina, who is married to Biagio, is both amused and perturbed by Nino's infatuation, as the boy arouses in her a maternal instinct that she has never been able to satisfy. A strange relationship grows up between the two, but when Cettina submits to the amorous approaches of Sasà, one of her husband's friends, Nino is bitterly jealous. Before long, though, the boy comes to accept reality: he marries his cousin, Giulietta, and makes a date with Cettina for the days to come.

REVIEWS

"A Sicilian middle-class environment, cut off from the contemporary world, provides the background to an adolescent's sexual awakening. A dangerous subject, that Bolognini handles with modesty and just the right touch. He never tries to compete with Visconti or Bertolucci... Too many slow-motion flash-backs, perhaps, too much insistence on the appearance of a "double" beside the boy; a sententious "double" is not enough, however, to dissipate the film's overall charm... Bolognini argues that the editing was tampered with, but there is little justification for his complaint that Gina Lollobrigida was forced upon him by the producers. Beautifully photographed by Nannuzzi, this 'autumn rose' challenges time, and is both amusing and in the end moving." (Gérard Legrand, *Positif*, n. 138, May 1972).

"Bolognini has made this film which, though recognizably adapted for the screen by the same hand as another

GINA LOLLOBRIGIDA
GABRIELE FERZETTI
ANDRE LAURENCE dans

ce merveilleux AUTOMNE

un film de
MAURO BOLOGNINI
d'après le roman de
ERCOLE PATTI
EASTMANCOLOR

United Artists

film about Sicily (Brancati's *Il bell-Antonio*), is unfortunately less convincing. Too much food put on the fire, and too much of it overdone. Although the photography is beautiful... the dialogue is graceless and clumsy, with merely a hint of the Sicilian accent to remind us where we are. As regards the acting, Gina Lollobrigida has little chance to show her skill, though she shows a lot of other things, in the role of the aunt." (Guglielmo Biraghi, *Il Messaggero*, 6 April 1969).

"...superb photography and art direction and a wonderful variety of types in the cast... [Bolognini] is hampered here by a script that reeks of old-fashioned melodrama, despite its modern setting, and poor casting in some major roles, especially the key role of Nino... Even the beautiful Gina, who could stir a sphinx to action, can't get more than a mooncalf look on the young man's face. (*Variety*, 23 June 1971).

Stuntman

1969

Produced by Turi Vasile for Ultra Film (Rome) and Marianne Productions (Paris). Director: Marcello Baldi. Story: Lucille Laks. Screenplay: Alessandro Continenza and Marcello Baldi. Photography: Carlo Carlini (Eastmancolor). Music: Carlo Rustichelli. Art director: Lucio Lucentini. Editor: Mario Morra. Distribution: Paramount. Origin: Italy/France. French title: *Le cascadeur*. Running time: 97 minutes.

CAST

Gina Lollobrigida (Evelyn Lake), Marisa Mell (Gloria), Robert Viharo (Johnny), Marie Dubois (Yvette), Paul Muller (Lamb), Jean-Claude Bercq (Omero), Giuseppe Lauricella (Baldi), Claudio Perone (Shorty), Aldo De Carellis (Bill), Carla Antonelli (Frau Heller), Benito Boggino (Pierre), Umberto Raho (Insurance company president), Marina Lando (Journalist), Dennis Hall (Lawyer), Sandre Pellegrini (Police inspector), Giuseppe Liuzzi (Exhibition director), Maria Pia Nardon (Secretary), Camilla Moser (Registrar), Virgilio Conti (Pierre's friend), Mimmo Poli, Paola Natale, Carla Foscari.

SYNOPSIS

Johnny, stuntman tired of risking his life in order to earn a living, decides that the best thing he could do would be to marry a rich woman. He tries his luck with much–married divorcee Evelyn Lake, but she prefers Bill, a wealthy old man confined to a wheelchair. He makes another equally unsuccessful attempt after which he turns his hand to robbery. Aided by Gloria, he steals a valuable statue and then tries to collect insurance on it. But his plans are thwarted by Yvette, a pretty young detective working on behalf of the insurance company, and he gets back to his old profession as a stuntman—and dating Yvette. In the meantime, Evelyn has been left a widow. She realizes that she has always loved Johnny, who dumps Yvette and accepts Evelyn's offer of marriage.

BACKGROUND AND REVIEWS

"The hero of our story is a penniless stuntman who tries to seduce a beautiful, wealthy divorcee—Gina

Lollobrigida in splendid form—bringing into play all the tricks of the trade. The story proceeds cheerfully through all manner of adventures...'La Lollo' works beside the engaging and talented Robert Viharo, who gives a convincing portrayal of Johnny, Marie Dubois, Jean-Claude Bercq, Marisa Mell and Paul Muller." (Vice, *Il Messaggero*, 11 April 1969).

"Frenzied Italian capers in which a few spectacular car-driving stunts pad out a plot as unmemorable and unappetizing as soggy spaghetti. Gina Lollobrigida is wasted as a money-grabbing divorcee, with little to do but chatter interminably about ex-husbands and large slabs of alimony." (*Monthly Film Bulletin,* March 1970).

...E continuavano a fregarsi il milione di dollari (Bad Man's River)

1970

Produced by Bernard Gordon for International Apollo Film—Zurbano Film—Jacques Roitfeld. Story and screenplay: Eugenio Martin and Philip Yordan. Photography: Alejandro Ulloa (Eastmancolor). Music: Waldo De Los Rios. Art director: Julio Molino. Editor: Antonio Ramirez De Loayra. Distribution: Fida Cinematografica. Origin: Spain/Italy/France. French title: *Les quatre mercenaires d'El Paso*. American title: *Bad Man's River*. Running time: 90 minutes.

CAST

Lee Van Cleef (Bomba), Gina Lollobrigida (Alicia), James Mason (Monedero), Gianni Garko (Pupo), Sergio Fantoni (Fierro), Jess Hahn (Odie), Simon Andreu (Angel), Diana Lorys (Dolores), Aldo Sanbrell (Canales), Luis Rivera (Orozco), Lone Ferk (Concita), Eduardo Fajardo (Duarte), Per Barclay (Reverend).

With James Mason and Lee Van Cleef.

With Lee Van Cleef.

SYNOPSIS

Bomba, a Texas bankrobber, is 'deprived' of a recent 'haul' by the beautiful but unscrupulous Alicia. He and his three companions then agree to work for a revolutionary named Monedero, and again meet Alicia, who is posing as Monedero's wife. Bomba completes the job for which he is not paid, but is promised a million dollars if he manages to steal this sum of money from a delegate of the Mexican government. He realizes, however, that Alicia has tricked him again. In fact, she and Monedero are hiding on a ship, waiting to collect the million dollars with a credit card. Bomba succeeds in getting the money, but at this point he, Alicia and Monedero are captured by the Mexicans, although soon freed when the Mexicans learn that they helped the revolutionaries. Alicia, up to her tricks again, enlists the help of Billy the Kid, who robs Bomba of his million dollars. Then she and the famous bandit run off together leaving Bomba and Monedero empty-handed!

BACKGROUND AND REVIEWS

Gina Lollobrigida even made a light-hearted spaghetti-western, but it was only a minor film. But there again, this particular category of movies seldom was very kind to actresses, not to Bardot nor Cardinale nor Moreau. Neither could one expect to find an exception in a co-production with Spain directed by such an old spaghetti-western hand as Eugenio Martin. Released on the quiet in 1972, the film has left no trace, except perhaps on American TV.

"The story as it unfolds is well-defined, the humor lively and amusing, for those who do not expect too much from a movie. It is well enough directed, but the true tone of the film is derived from the active participation of such agreeable actors as Lee Van Cleef, James Mason, not to mention a still very attractive Gina Lollobrigida." (Vice, *Il Messaggero*, 29 January 1972).

"*Bad Man's River* goes under wasting the talents of Gina Lollobrigida and James Mason." (*The Guardian*).

Le avventure di Pinocchio (Pinocchio)

1971

Produced by Sanpaolo Film, Cinepat. Una esclusività International Film Company. Executive producer: Attilio Monge. Director: Luigi Comencini. Adapted from the book by Carlo Collodi. Screenplay: Luigi Comencini and Suso Cecchi D'Amico. Photography: Armando Nannuzzi (Technicolor). Music: Fiorenzo Carpi. Art director: Pietro Gherardi. Costumes: Arrigo Breschi. Editor: Nino Baragli. Distribution: MGM. Origin: Italy.

The credits refer to the screen version which followed the five-episode television edition that was co-produced by RAI-Radiotelevisione Italiana (Turin), O.R.T.F. (Paris), Bavaria Film (Munich), in cooperation with Sanpaolo Film (Rome).

CAST

Andrea Balestri (Pinocchio), Nino Manfredi (Geppetto), Gina Lollobrigida (Lovely little girl with blue hair), Franco Franchi (Cat), Ciccio Ingrassia (Fox), Ugo D'Alessio (Master Cherry), Lionel Stander (Fire eater), Vittorio De Sica (Judge), Mario Adorf (Ringmaster), Enzo Cannavale (Owner of the 'Inn of the Red Crayfish'), Domenico Santore (Candlewick), Riccardo Billi (Cartman), Zoe Incrocci (Snail), Pietro Gentili and Mimmo Olivieri (Carabinieri), Carmine Torre (Fisherman), Vera Drudi (Fire eater's wife), Orazio Orlando ("Brigadiere"), Marie Scaccia and Jacques Herlin (Doctors), Carlo Bagne (Melampo's owner), Giuseppe Caffarelli (First carabiniere), Furio Meniconi (Countryman), Galliano Sbarra (Thief in prison), Nerina Montagnani (Marten), Caporali (Cockle seller), Siria Betti (Candlewick's mother), Mario Cardarelli (Fruit seller), Luigi Leoni (Schoolmaster), Clara Colosimo (Shopowner at the port), Pino Ferrara and Roberto Pistoni (Fishermen), Luigi De Ritis (Carabiniere), Carlo Colombaioni (Donkey seller), Mario Ercolani, Bruno Bassi, Giovanna Lucci, Willy Semmelrogge, Mario Narcisi, Antonio Danesi, Orlando Dubaldo, Natale Siddi, Simone Santo, Fred Pistoni, Nazzareno Caldarelli, Ferdinando Murolo and the puppets of the Teatro Colla of Milan.

The story is very similar to that of Collodi's book, although certain minor characters are made more important, especially in the film. As regards Pinocchio himself, he is played by a boy who only on rare occasions turns into a wooden puppet.

Wrote Collodi: "And a lovely little girl appeared at the window, with blue hair, a face as white as a wax image, her eyes closed, her hands crossed on her breast; without moving her lips, she said in a voice that seemed to come from another world: 'Is there nobody in this house—Is everybody dead?'"

BACKGROUND AND REVIEWS

Lollobrigida, in an interview with the daily *Paese Sera* on 8 April 1972, remarked: "I am very satisfied with my role. While we were filming I seemed to have a magical power over children, who watched me with admiration and respect. The film's modernity lies in the fact that I am no longer a good fairy, but a mother. A mother like thousands of others, concerned for her undisciplined child. And to make the character even more up-to-date, my clothes are very simple. The only extravagant and unusual thing about me is my fabulous turquoise wig."

But not all the critics enjoyed her portrayal. Certainly not Ivano Cipriani of *Paese Sera* who (on 16 April 1972) wrote: "Rather weak, however, is Gina Lollobrigida-the Fairy," and on 23 April, he added: "The scenes in which the Fairy-Gina Lollobrigida appears are certainly insipid, especially in view of the distance separating the actress from the character she has to play." While Ugo Buzzolan remarked in *La Stampa* on 23 April 1972: " 'La Lollo' is the fairy (in the color version) because she has a turquoise wig, but there is little else magical about her; she is a good woman, no longer in her prime, honest and shapely still, an experienced housewife of a middle-class background, a virtuous lady who does charity work, who can play the harp and sing." He later added: "The place where everyone works hard and where

the good fairy, Gina Lollobrigida—who is just right in the role created for her by the teleplay writers of a middle-class lady who delights in charity work—dispenses food to the poor with celestial zeal. Anyway, here is Pinocchio once again in the good fairy's haven (which, between you and me, is more like a garçconniere for Victorian gentlemen, than the dwelling of a gentle and presumably chaste creature who presumably is not of this world)."

With David Niven.

Un ospite gradito…per mia moglie (King, Queen, Knave)

1972

Produced by David L. Wolper for Maran Film and Wolper Pictures Ltd. Director: Jerzy Skolimowski. From the novel *Korol, Dama, Valet* by Vladimir Nabokov. Screenplay: David Seltzer and David Shaw. Photography: Charly Steinberger (Eastmancolor). Music: Stanley Meyers. Art director: Rolf Zehtbauer. Editor: Mel Shapiro. Distribution: Independenti Regonali. Origin: Federal Germany/USA. Running time: 92 minutes. English title: *King, Queen, Knave*. French title: *Roi, dame, valet*. German title: *Herzbube*.

CAST

Gina Lollobrigida (Martha Dreyer), David Niven (Charles Dreyer), John Moulder Brown (Frank Dreyer), Mario Adorf (Ritter), Carl-Fox Duering (Entricht), Christopher Sandford (Hofmann), Christine Schuberth (Isolda), Felicitas Peters (Ida), Erica Beer (Frieda), Elma Karlowa (Hanna), Morgens von Gadow (Piffke).

SYNOPSIS

Frank Dreyer, a 19-year-old who has lost his parents in an accident, moves to Munich to stay with his aunt and uncle, Martha and Charles Dreyer. Avaricious Martha is attracted by Frank's youthful vitality and, after having coaxed him out of his initial shyness becomes his mistress. After awhile, the two lovers work out a plan to get rid of Charles in a boating "accident." Suddenly, Charles stumbles on a scheme that will make a fortune, and Martha has second thoughts, deciding that her love of money is greater than her love for Frank! Unfortunately, it is too late to turn back, but because of Martha's hesitation the plan backfires and it is she—a non-swimmer like Charles—who ends up in the water. Uncle and nephew are left to enjoy their newly acquired wealth.

With David Niven.

BACKGROUND AND REVIEWS

Skolimowski's film was Gina Lollobrigida's last as a top box office name. She speaks of it with regret, as though it were an occasion wasted. The name of the author of the novel from which the film was taken (Nabokov), that of the director, who had made such films as *Rysopis* (1964), *Walkover* (1965), *Deep End* (1970), and the cast themselves, promised well indeed.

It has far more vulgar dialogue than the original, and the reputation of having been a failure. Even Skolimowski speaks of it as a totally negative experience: "It's a horrible movie... With film-ing over, I soon became fed up with fighting the editor, a typical Hollywood editor who had been forced on us by the American producers. There was some good material to begin with, there was all of Nabokov's irony and ruthless-ness. But it was impossible to put it all together in an intelligent manner with someone on the telephone all the time to his bosses in Los Angeles telling them what I was planning to do...After two or three weeks of working like this I gave up and left them to it...I was amazed when I learned later that the film had been presented at the Cannes Film Festival." (Interviewed by Michel Ciment, *Positif*, n. 214, January 1979).

"It would have been hard to predict that David Niven, Gina Lollobrigida and John Moulder Brown would have teamed so brilliantly in Skolimowski's idiosyncratic style of farce." (*The London Times*).

"...an intermittently funny black comedy on first love, avariciousness, and underneath, a subversive look at economic booms and woman relations in the upper classes...[the] sexy aunt [is] Gina Lollobrigida (in top mature look)...there are some hilarious love love scenes as Miss Lollobrigida teaches the fledgling the ropes." (Mosk., *Variety*, 24 May 1972).

Peccato mortale (Mortal Sin)

1972

Produced by C. P. Cinematografica (Rome) – Hildago A. Valasco (Madrid) – Les Productions du Bassau (Paris). Director: Francisco Rovira-Beleta. From the novel *No encontre rosas para ma madre* by José Antonio Garcia Blasquez. Screenplay: J. A. Garcia Blasquez, André Velasco, Corrado Cuoco, Enrico Josa, Paul Andreota, F. Rovira-Beleta. Photography: Michel Kleber (Technicolor). Music: Piero Piccioni, Editor: Gianfranco Amicucci. Distribution: Indipendenti Regionali. Origin: Spain/France/Italy. French title: *Roses rouges et piments verts*. Spanish title: *Ye no he hallado las rosas para mi madre*. American title: *The Lonely Woman*.

CAST

Renaud Verley (Jasi), Susan Hampshire (Elaine), Danielle Darrieux (Teresa, Jasi's mother), Gina Lollobrigida (Netty), Giacomo Rossi Stuart (Richard Leighton), Conchita Valasco, Maribel Martin, Javier Loyola.

Note: According to the original credits, Gina Lollobrigida was making a "guest appearance."

On some of the posters advertising the Italian version, the title was preceded by the following phrase: "To use violence on a minor is a mortal sin."

SYNOPSIS

Jasi is a young Spanish boy with a mother-fixation and he'll go to any lengths to please her. Jobless, he becomes the lover of a rich photographer, Netty, at the same time posing for her husband, a painter of dubious repute. Then, with the help of a girlfriend, Elaine, he plans to stage Netty's abduction, but the photographer learns of the plot and throws him out. Instead, Jasi marries a millionairess and with money now no object, he is able to buy his mother fabulous presents, including a splendid villa. She, however, no longer has any need, having found herself a rich lover.

BACKGROUND AND REVIEWS

"The confused story of a young scoundrel afflicted by a sort of Oedipus complex...Everything that takes place on the screen is totally gratuitous and in any case is difficult to understand." (Vice, *Il Messaggero*, 8 June 1975).

"The story of an unpleasant young man suffering from an Oedipus complex of considerable proportions who becomes involved with married women and young girls alike, but with his mind on his mother all the time. Directed by Spain's Rovira-Beleta, the film has a cosmopolitan cast, for what it is worth, including France's Renaud Verley and Danielle Darrieux, Britain's Susan Hampshire and Italy's Gina Lollobrigida...The result is nonetheless horribly provincial." (Anonymous, *L'Unità*, 8 June 1975).

With Renaud Verley.

140

GINA LOLLOBRIGIDA ON TELEVISION

Il Mattatore

1959

Gina Lollobrigida made a guest appearance in one episode of Vittorio Gassman's programe *Il mattatore* in the part of a muddle-headed film star. Commented Gina in an interview: "In all my career I have never received so much praise. And what was the reason? Because I created a caricature of an unnamed film star and everyone took her to be me. If there ever was an illiterate, bungling actress, who could it be if not 'La Lollo'? And so I agreed to play the role of the foolish film star, and afterwards the critics wrote eagerly that I had been superb, that the sketch was so amusing, just right for me, audacious, etc. When we were doing the one and only rehearsal on television and got to the point where the film star, having forgotten her lines, fumbles desperately in her handbag in search of the piece of paper on which she has scribbled down a few reminders, I felt a wave of hostility and commiseration from those around. Everyone, electricians and technicians alike, thought that I had really forgotten my lines. Then they caught on and began to laugh..." (Interview edited by Gianfranco Calderoni, *Successo*, year I, n. I, May 1959).

Stasera Gina Lollobrigida

1969

Directed by Antonello Falqui. Dialogue: Marchesi, Terzoli, Vaime. Conductor: Bruno Canfora. Choreography: Don Lurio. Art director: Cesarini da Senegallia. Costumes: Corrado Colabucci. Executive producer: Guido Sacerdoti. Running time: 75 minutes.

In "Tonight Gina Lollobrigida."

Gina Lollobrigida, Alberto Sordi, Vittorio De Sica.

Notes: The show was televised by a state channel on 24 May 1969. One of the male dancers was Pietro Valpreda, an anarchist, later suspected of terrorist activity in Italy.

The show consisted of musical numbers, guest appearances (Sordi and De Sica) and a series of sketches in which Lollobrigida played a number of famous women from the past—Cleopatra, Eleonora Duse, Josephine Baker, Marie Walewska, Helen of Troy, George Sand, Lucretia Borgia and Tereskowa.

Gina Lollobrigida has also appeared on a number of American television variety shows, among them *The Dean Martin Show*, *The Sammy Davis Show*, *The Engelbert Humperdinck Show* and *The Bob Hope Show*.

In September 1970, she was engaged for one episode of the series *The Name of the Game*, starring Robert Stack and Anthony Franciosa. The episode was entitled *Una suora napolitana* (A Neapolitan Nun). But there was a disagreement with the producers and Gina left the film, her role being taken by Geraldine Page.

In 1971 Gina starred in the five episodes of *Le avventure di Pinocchio*, which was later adapted for the screen and is described in the preceding chapter.

Finally making her American television acting debut in November 1984, Lollobrigida played Francesca Gioberti, a wealthy but financially-strapped Italian vintner who comes to America to make things difficult for her half sister, Angela Channing (played by Jane Wyman) in five episodes of *Falcon Crest*.

Subsequently, she had a leading role in the four-hour television movie, *Deceptions*, in 1985.

With Enzo Tortora in "Tonight Gina Lollobrgida."

Deceptions

(1985)

Directed by Robert Chenault and Melville Shavelson.
A Louis Rudolph production. Executive producer, Louis Rudolph; producer, William Hill; teleplay: Melville Shavelson, from the novel by Judith Michael; photography: Ernest Day and Jack Atcheler; editors: Bill Blunden, Brian Smedley-Aston and Alan Pattillo; music: Nigel Hess; production designer, John Blezard. Running time: 4 hours (in 2 parts).

CAST

Stefanie Powers (Sabrina Longworth/ Stephanie Richards), Barry Bostwick (Grant Richards), Jeremy Brett (Bryan Foxworth), James Faulkner (Richard Blackwell), Sam Wanamaker (Jim Nolan), Fabio Testi (Carlo Ferraro), John Woodvine (Chief Inspector), Joan Sims (Mrs. Thirkell), Fairuza Balk (Penny Richards), Brenda Vaccaro (Helen Adams), Gina Lollobrigida (Princess Alessandra).

In this dramatization of Judith Michael's best-selling novel about identical twin sisters—an unhappy housewife in suburban New Jersey and a European jet-setter—who decide to change identities—and lives—for a week (both are played by Stefanie Powers). Gina Lollobrigida is the continental sister's beautiful and wealthy Italian Confidente. Filming was done entirely on location in England and Italy.

The Citadel Press Film Series

From James Stewart to Moe Howard and the Three Stooges, Woody Allen to John Wayne,
The Citadel Press Film Series is America's largest film book library.
Now with more than 100 titles in print, books in the series make perfect gifts--
for a loved one, a friend, or yourself!

The Films of...

Alan Ladd
Alfred Hitchcock
All Talking! All Singing!
  All Dancing!
Anthony Quinn
The Bad Guys
Barbara Stanwyck
Barbra Streisand:
  The First Decade
Barbra Streisand:
  The Second Decade
Bela Lugosi
Bette Davis
Bing Crosby
Boris Karloff
Bowery Boys
Brigitte Bardot
Burt Reynolds
Carole Lombard
Cary Grant
Cecil B. DeMille
Character People
Charles Bronson
Charlie Chaplin
Charlton Heston
Clark Gable
Classics of the Gangster
  Film
Classics of the Horror Film
Classics of the Silent Screen
Cliffhanger
Clint Eastwood
Curly: Biography of a
  Superstooge
David Niven
Detective in Film
Dick Tracy
Doris Day
Dustin Hoffman
Elizabeth Taylor

Elvis Presley
Errol Flynn
Federico Fellini
The Fifties
The Forties
Forgotten Films to Remember
Frank Sinatra
Fredric March
Fritz Lang
Gary Cooper
Gene Kelley
Gina Lollobrigida
Ginger Rogers
Gloria Swanson
Great Adventure Films
Great British Films
Great French Films
Great German Films
Great Romantic Films
Great Spy Films
Gregory Peck
Greta Garbo
Harry Warren and the
  Hollywood Musical
Hedy Lamarr
Henry Fonda
Hollywood Cheesecake:
  60 Years of Leg Art
Hollywood's Hollywood
Howard Hughes in Hollywood
Humphrey Bogart
Ingrid Bergman
Jack Lemmon
Jack Nicholson
James Cagney
James Mason
Jane Fonda
Jeanette MacDonald and
  Nelson Eddy
Jean Harlow

Jewish Image in American
  Film
Joan Crawford
John Garfield
John Huston
John Wayne
John Wayne Reference
  Book
Judy Garland
Katharine Hepburn
Kirk Douglas
Lana Turner
Laurel and Hardy
Lauren Bacall
Laurence Olivier
Lost Films of the
  Fifties
Love in the Film
Mae West
Marilyn Monroe
Marlene Dietrich
Marlon Brando
Moe Howard and the
  Three Stooges
Montgomery Clift
More Character People
More Classics of the
  Horror Film
Myrna Loy
Non-Western Films of
  John Ford
Olivia de Havilland
Paul Newman
Peter Lorre
Pictorial History of Science
  Fiction Films
Pictorial History of Sex
  in Films
Pictorial History of War
  Films

Pictorial History of the
  Western Film
Rebels: The Rebel Hero
  in Films
Rita Hayworth
Robert Redford
Robert Taylor
Ronald Colman
Ronald Reagan
The Seventies
Sex in the Movies
Sci-Fi 2
Sherlock Holmes
Shirley MacLaine
Shirley Temple
The Sixties
Sophia Loren
Spencer Tracy
Steve McQueen
Susan Hayward
Tarzan of the Movies
They Had Faces Then
The Thirties
Those Glorious Glamour Years
Three Stooges Book of Scripts
Three Stooges Book of Scripts,
  Vol. 2
The Twenties
20th Century Fox
Tyrone Power
Warren Beatty
W.C. Fields
Western Films of John Ford
William Holden
William Powell
Woody Allen
World War II

Ask for these titles at your bookseller. And send for our listing with prices:
Citadel Press, 120 Enterprise Avenue, Secaucus, New Jersey 07094.